Outlands

OUTLANDS

*Journeys to the Outer Edges
of Cape Cod*

BY

Robert Finch

David R. Godine · Publisher

BOSTON

First published in 1986 by
DAVID R. GODINE, *Publisher*
Post Office Box 450
Jaffrey, New Hampshire 03452
www.godine.com

Some of these essays originally appeared, in somewhat different
form, in the following publications: "An Alewife Lesson" and
"Star People" in Blair & Ketchum's Country Journal; *"A Summer*
Place" in Orion Nature Quarterly; *"The Tactile Land"*
and "A Beach for All Seasons" in Sanctuary;
and "Nighttracking" in Diversion.

Library of Congress Cataloging-in-Publication Data

Finch, Robert, 1943–
Outlands: journeys to the outer edges of Cape Cod.
1. Natural history—Massachusetts—Cape Cod.
2. Cape Cod (Mass.) I. Title.
QH105.M4F565 1986   508.744'92   85-45972
ISBN 0-87923-742-2

SECOND SOFTCOVER PRINTING 2002
Printed in Canada

For my father and mother,
Charles Wesley and Fritzi Wasserburger Finch,
with love

Contents

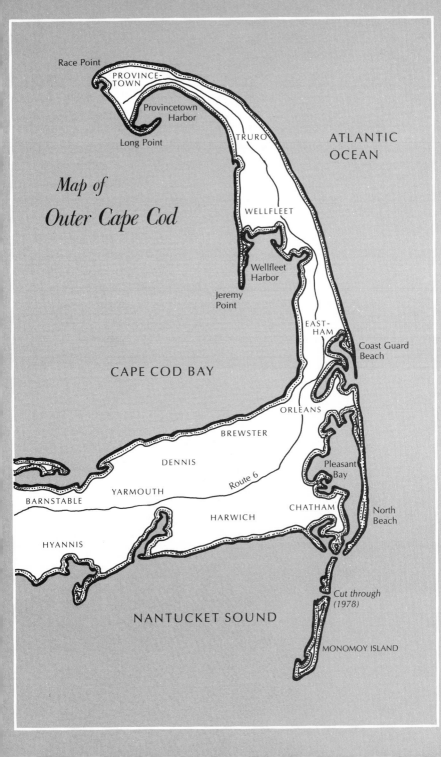

Map of
Outer Cape Cod

Race Point
PROVINCE-
TOWN
Provincetown
Harbor
TRURO
Long Point
ATLANTIC
OCEAN
WELLFLEET
Wellfleet
Harbor
Jeremy
Point
EAST-
HAM
Coast Guard
Beach
CAPE COD BAY
ORLEANS
BREWSTER
DENNIS
Pleasant
Bay
Route 6
YARMOUTH
BARNSTABLE
CHATHAM
North
Beach
HARWICH
HYANNIS
Cut through
(1978)
NANTUCKET SOUND
MONOMOY ISLAND

Outlands

One That Got Away

THIS IS SOMETHING in the nature of a confession, I suppose. But the trouble is that even now, long after the event, I am still not sure what it is I have to confess: a recklessness or a cowardice, a sin of commission or omission, a drama of ultimate limits or a trivial matter of twenty minutes and a leaky boot.

I have some idea of what might have brought it on. It may have had something to do with a dream I had the night before, or with a certain feeling of self-containment that had grown upon me as an oppression during the previous week. . . .

But since, even at this distance, I am still not sure *what* occurred, there is little point in analyzing motives or rationalizing behavior beforehand. Let me simply try to describe the incident as it happened and see what emerges. And you, reader, keep your distance a little from the narrative. Do not get too caught up in what I am trying to remember. Do not listen too closely to the shifts and withdrawals of emotion that underlie and

3

punctuate its progress. Imagine yourself, if you will, raised up above the action, a little like gods, perhaps, or in a stadium, or on one of those hills on which generals used to stand to watch the clash of their armies in the valleys below. Keep your eye on the movements, and let that tell you what happened, more than whatever cries or shouts of combat come up from below.

It happened in late February. There had been continuous rains, heavy at times, and strong easterly gale winds throughout the weekend. That morning the weather, though still wet and gusty, was mild and misty. It seemed like a good day to drive up to Eastham and watch the ocean overwash the barrier spit at Coast Guard Beach. Storm breakthroughs at this beach had become a regular, even a familiar and anticipated event since a great winter northeaster had first ripped its dune ridge to shreds the winter before. Conditions once more seemed ripe for a breakthrough. High course tides were due just before noon, in conjunction with a partial solar eclipse—part of the last total eclipse of the sun over North America for another thirty-eight years. Things seemed propitious.

I put on my rain gear and headed for Coast Guard Beach, arriving about 10:30 A.M. Already a crowd of cars had begun to gather in the storm overlook area behind the old Coast Guard station. At the bottom of the hill was the former site of the beach's parking lot. Slightly more than a year ago, record storm surges had ripped up its asphalt and demolished the bathhouse, yet now it looked as if there had never been anything there but beach.

It was nearly an hour and a half to high tide, but already the salt marsh behind the long barrier spit had turned into a broad dark-blue lake, beating against the mainland shore to the west. Wide, thick mats of muddy foam were strewn about on the marsh side of the beach, washed over on last night's tide. Several of the snow fences placed across the cut to trap sand had been flattened and carried away, but some had miraculously held. Beyond the cut, the long, ravaged spit of Coast Guard Beach stretched a mile and a half southward, but it was too misty to see any of the remaining beach cottages from the overlook, to tell if any of them had been hit again. And to the east there loomed the cause of it all, the great advancing storm-tossed ocean, erupting majestically upon the beach, while legions of sullen, determined clouds raced inland overhead. It was a day to be careful what you asked the flounder.

The occupants of the dozen or so cars in the parking area remained inside, so I decided to take the opportunity to have an unimpeded view of the storm at close range. Pulling on a pair of waders and buttoning up my slicker, I got out and walked down the hill toward the beach, shrouded in wind-driven mist and spray. As I stood at the bottom of the blocked-off road, watching great cascades of white foam piling up onto the beach, I could see that the next series of overwashes had already begun. The tops of the crashing swells were just beginning to urge themselves up over the hump of the upper beach, spilling down the long sloping backside toward the marsh. So far they were only shallow sheens and braided little rivulets of water, but they gave notice that a wide salt river would soon course through here again at high tide.

On the far side of the destroyed lower parking lot, standing at the base of the foredunes just above the reach of the surf, was the silhouette of a very large gull, its head bent down, eating something on the beach. I walked closer to the cut-through to see better, and as I did it grew into the rounded, hull-shaped body of a white goose. I stood marveling: could it be a snow goose? Then, as I fumbled for my binoculars, the rain let up and the mist cleared momentarily; the white form loomed larger still, uncurled an incredibly long neck up into the air, and blossomed into the improbable but unmistakable shape of a swan.

What on earth was a *swan* doing here on the Outer Beach in the middle of a raging northeaster? What had brought it here, and what had it been eating? Its appearance seemed avatarlike and strangely compelling. It was, I realized, hidden from view to those in the cars up on the hill. I thought of waving them down to see it, but before I could, the bird turned its head toward me, unsheathed its huge white wings, and sailed low and quickly, like some enormous milkweed seed, down the length of the beach in front of the dune ridge and out of sight.

Rain and mist swirled again, but I looked through the binoculars to see if the swan might have landed farther down the beach. Where it had been, the beach seemed to have shaped itself to the storm, forming a perfectly smooth curving battlement up which the breakers ran halfway, doing little dances, and rolling back. But further down, the waves were already crashing into vertical sand walls four or five feet high, foaming for several seconds into an element neither land nor sea, but both, and carrying visible sections of dune away with each sucking withdrawal. The tops of the low dune walls cracked and slid, and the long, naked pale-yellow roots of beach grass trailed down into the foamy water like strands of rock kelp pulled seaward on granite shores. There was no sign of the swan.

I could also see now, through moving rips in the mist, two of the three surviving cottages on the far side. One was heavily damaged and precariously exposed at the north end of the dune ridge, but the second, a bit farther down and set back from the beach, still sat relatively secure and untouched in a hollow just behind one of the few undamaged dunes.

And as I watched, a thought, one that had been growing slowly and unawares in the back of my mind for the past several minutes, now suddenly surged forward and seized me in a rush: *I would cross over.*

It came, not as a decision, but as a fully formed conviction. I knew what I was going to do. And more: I knew exactly how I was going to do it, as though I had been unconsciously preparing for it all morning and was now simply giving a final review to my plans. I would cross the open plain of the cut to the far side before the washovers grew any deeper or more frequent. I already had everything I needed: my slicker and waders would keep me dry, and in my pocket was a stale jelly doughnut. There, on the last remaining stretch of high dunes on Coast Guard Beach, I would spend the duration of the high tide, alone with the three cottages, the swan, and the storm. It was a good storm, but not big enough to pose any serious threat to my safety. The tide would subside by four o'clock, five at the latest, giving me plenty of time to get back across before dark. It was enough. I was ready.

It looked easy enough. The rain had let up, the mist had cleared. It was, at most, a minute's run, even in waders, across the wide, smooth plain of the overwash area to the storm-ravaged barrier spit.

I walked over to the edge of the former parking lot, where the sand was highest and some snow fencing still remained. To the east the storm waves were now beginning to crest over the top of the beach, spilling down the backslope and sinking into the sands before they reached the flooded marsh behind. In front of me the water ran by in rapid little channels, only a few inches deep and a few yards wide. Beyond them, a clear, flat plain of moist sand. And beyond that, the eroding dunes, the surviving cottages, the apparition of the white swan, and the solitude of the storm.

Piece of cake, as they say. Yet I knew I had better not hesitate; the tide was still coming in, and very soon the overwashes would begin in earnest. Also, the impulsive adventurer today always hears at his back the government official hovering near: though there were no signs around saying "Do Not Cross Over During Storms," a Seashore ranger might show up at any moment and order me ignominiously off the beach.

So, without further thought, I set off confidently across the first of the small channels—and instantly received a shock, more of surprise than cold, as my right foot filled with icy seawater. I looked down: there was a slit in the waders, a small tear less than a half-inch long just above the ankle. *Damn!* I thought, *Damn it anyway!* There goes comfort, there goes protection, there goes everything. For however appealing the romantic scenario I had been fashioning for myself, I had no intention of spending several hours out on a barrier beach with a cold, soaked foot.

I stood, thwarted, on the far side of the first channel I had just crossed, staring down with anger and frustration at the small but decisive chink in my armor. Looking back up at the cars parked behind the old Coast Guard station, I saw that they had grown in number and now lined the road that sloped down the hill toward the beach. If I did not want to be an uncomfortable adventurer, neither did I want to be just one of them, a mere observer, a spectator of spectacles.

The desire and promise of the storm rose before me again. I wanted to be part of it, to experience the obliteration of this long beach, not from some heightened perspective, but from inside; to be out there riding the bare dune ridge into the foamy teeth of destruction, to feel the sand shake beneath me with each onslaught of the sea, to watch the muddy surges gouge and slice off clumps of beach grass from around my feet. Perhaps I might even get to see one of the three remaining cottages nudged off its foundations and sent sidling and waddling, like some ungainly hippopotamus, down into the flooded marsh.

I had to get across, but the soaked foot, as cold as reality, still held me back. Then I had an idea: I might be able to hop across these deeper but narrow channels on one leg, keeping my leaky foot in the air, and still manage to get across relatively dry. It would be a less than graceful crossing, but it seemed so silly, so *stupid*, to be turned back at this point by something as trivial as a leaky boot. At any rate, I had to try.

Stepping back and taking a short run, I did manage to skip successfully across the second channel on one foot, and from there strode determinedly out across the lower rounded plain of the cut-through. But as I did, a low, wide surge of water came up over the crest of the beach and began to roll toward me. At first it looked like a mere sheen of water upon the sand, but when it reached me it was about eight inches deep. Still, I managed to keep hopping in place while it passed, or rather, nearly in place, for with each jump I found myself nudged gently backward toward the marsh by the force of the shallow current.

After the surge had gone by, I trotted back to higher ground, where I stopped and stood again, facing the cut. Once more it was only a plain of wet sand, but this time I knew the truth. If I were to get across to the barrier island, I would not get there dry. The shallow surges, which had looked like mere skins of water from here, were deeper than they seemed. I cursed the cheap Japanese waders I wore and wished (with the trite hell of mundane truth seen too late) that I had brought along my good pair. But there was no time to go back for them now—and perhaps it was too late in any case. I asked myself if a little stupid cold water was going to stop me, and found myself answering, yes, I guessed it was.

So, resigned to discretion, I started up from the beach, and as I did I became aware of what a curious and conspicuous sight I must have presented to the cars above: a man, dressed in a red-orange slicker and waders, hopping on one foot back and forth across the beach. What did they think of me, all those watchers on the hill? What did they make of all my indecisive comings and goings? Did they think I was dancing, or did they divine what I was up to? And if they did, did they cheer me or chastise me in their minds?

I began to feel not so much like a dissatisfied or frustrated spectator, but like a performer in an arena, one who was not only testing himself but carrying with him the expectations and vicarious aspirations of the crowd. Strangely, people still remained in their cars, though the rain had virtually stopped. Were they, perhaps, mesmerized by my efforts? Did they think that by coming out now they might discourage me, break my resolve? Their staying inside began to seem a sort of vote of confidence, a silent encouragement, a sign that the outcome still lay in the balance. The people watching on the hill, warm and dry inside their vehicles, became not a threat but an inspiration and a responsibility. I found myself thinking that, after all, the water inside my right boot was not that bad. Already my body heat had warmed it up, creating a wet-suit effect that would actually act as insulation against subsequent soakings.

I turned back. Across the cut the truncated hulk of eroding dune cradled its diminishing collection of moribund structures in the face of the storm. It gained a renewed and intense desirability, commensurate with its vulnerability and increasing inaccessibility. A situation like this might come again, but never this opportunity, never this moment. I longed for the sea change it offered, but first I had to cross over to it, on its terms, not mine. I was being kept off only by a barrier of my own making, a petty fear of cold, wet feet. But what was a little physical discomfort in exchange for such a rare chance?

I began racing out across the overwash plain, knowing this time I would not turn back, splashing heedlessly through the shallow channels, out over the rounded sea-washed plain. I no longer cared what would happen once I reached that island, only that I wanted to be there, to become for an afternoon's space part of that good destruction, a witness and human measure of its uncircumferenced power.

I ran on, my feet splashing and leaving little pools behind in the wet sand, my wader legs slapping against one another rhythmically, as the dunes and their little cottages grew ever closer, ever more possible, ever more real. And then, nearly halfway across, I saw, too late, that I had misjudged again. A major surge lifted itself

up over the crest of the beach to my left and began to
roll straight across the cut at right angles to my own
progress. I knew I could not outrace it, that I had to stop
short and brace myself broadside to the surge, or I would
be knocked over and swamped. Even so, when it hit, I
felt the force of the water moving me, sliding me back,
back and down toward the marsh. The sand itself began
to slide with me under my feet, and I thought of the VW
that had been swept, driverless, off the parking lot and
out into the marsh on the night of the great storm a year
ago. The overwash was itself half water and half sand.
The grains sparkled and glsitened like stars as they
tumbled and fell around me. The water began to pour
into another tear in my waders, larger and higher up
around my thighs, and I felt it clutch at my groin with a
deep chill.

Hang on, hang on, was all I thought as the surge continued to rise and push against me. I could see only water
flowing around me now, and had the strange sensation
that I was not being pushed backward, but rather was
rushing headlong toward the seething ocean beyond, an
ocean which, as in a dream, did not get any closer as I
rushed forward, but even seemed to be receding.

The surge had crested to my waist now, pushing with
a steady but immeasurable force. Only my concentration
on keeping my balance kept me from giving way to panic,
though somewhere, far below, I was still convinced I
was in no real danger. In summer, meeting such a swell
head-on would have been great fun; but this was no play;
this was cold primal power, this was the end to all rules
and all options, the ultimate naysayer and decision maker.
And when I finally felt myself stop moving, when I
sensed that the force, the pulse of the surge, had rolled

past and the waters had begun to subside, I also knew which way I would go. . . .

But I went back laughing, partly from relief, but also with a strange sense of elation. I knew I would now have to be satisfied with a rather tame view of the flood from the secure battlements on the hill. I also knew I could likely have made it across before the next swell caught me; and, if not, it had only been the delay of my earlier hesitations that now made the crossing impossible.

Still, I had at least made a full effort, and in so doing had perhaps come closer to what I aimed at than I had really intended. And if in the end I was turned back, at least it had not been by considerations of human comfort, nor by official interference, nor even by what it would now have been much too easy to call common sense, but by the overwhelming and undeniable authority of that time and tide which, as ever, wait for no man.

As I climbed back up the hill, I passed the line of idling cars parked along the roadside. None of the occupants gave any sign they had been watching me, except for one man who, rolling down his window, remarked in a noncommittal tone, "I thought you were fishing out there."

I wanted to say that I was, and that the big one had gotten away. But the truth is, it just proved too big and I cut bait.

The Tactile Land

*I probably look at it [the moon] more now
than I did when I was younger. It's probably because I see a different thing than I
saw earlier. I used to see a disc in the sky
and now I see places—places I've been
and can relate to.*

—Neil Armstrong on the tenth anniversary
of the first moon walk

S EVERAL YEARS AGO, shortly before the birth
of my second child, I sat in the waiting room of a
maternity clinic in Plymouth, Massachusetts. My eyes
happened to fall on a young expectant mother across the
room as she reached out and, in a purely unconscious
gesture, casually caressed the head of her little boy just
behind his ear. Both the woman and her child were
strangers to me, but because I had performed that same
unconscious parental gesture hundreds of times, I not
only saw the movement of her hand, but felt it, felt the

curve of the child's head, the fine texture of the hair, the swirl and dip of the crown, the hollow behind the ear, the small, soft, fleshy fold of earlobe. From unpremeditated and forgotten affection there now rose, with this sight, palpable ripples of remembered feeling, tactile memories surfacing to color, warm, and vivify this simple visual scene. It was real to me, this tracing of the child's head by the mother; it enriched not only the present moment, but gave back to me parts of my own life that had gone unrecognized at the time.

That was the first time I became strongly aware of the great difference between merely observing an action or a scene and seeing it infused with the memory of tactile and emotional sensation. Drugs and danger, we are told, can heighten or expand the senses, but it seems to me that life is vivid to us primarily insofar as we have previously insinuated ourselves into it, so that it gives us back a part of ourselves as we behold it in others, in just such numerous, characteristically small ways.

This is as true of landscapes as of human intercourse, and may go far toward explaining what we mean when we speak, somewhat vaguely and self-deprecatingly, about those vanished rural inhabitants who lived "closer to the land" than we do. It is not that our ancestors were any more dependent upon the land or sea than we are, but they possessed a sense of direct, repetitive involvement, not only of remembered processes, but of the remembered texture that they brought to life's activities, which in turn gave them a strong feeling of identification with the land—a literal "sense of place."

It is true, of course, that it was in many ways a very narrow sense. On Cape Cod a life of subsistence farming or fishing demanded that the inhabitants see and know the landscape primarily in terms of extracting a living from it. Thus, consciously at least, they were likely to look at a salt marsh as a source of cattle fodder or shore-brids for market; a stranding of blackfish as a windfall of whale oil; a stand of oak as so many cords of firewood; or a cedar swamp as the site of a cranberry bog. Because of this, they often laid waste the landscape with a carelessness, even a vengeance, that the most inveterate city-dweller would find inexcusable today. Nature was no object to be contemplated from all sides in a detached manner, but a part of their lives and livelihood, to be entered directly into and without too much attention to the niceties.

Still, if their viewpoint was no less utilitarian than ours and their methods were more blatantly insensitive, they still needed an intimate physical knowledge of nature to survive. Every sight came to mean something in terms of tactile effort, of a task at once anticipated and remembered, whether it was the sun shining on a field of oats ready to be mowed, the tide running out over a full weir net, or a clear autumn sky filled with stars that meant a possible frost, so that the cranberry bogs would have to be watched over, and possibly flooded, into the night.

Rarely did these country people, these rural New Englanders, experience an aesthetic apprehension of their surroundings unyoked to some task or necessity it signified, and yet because of this the landscape was palpable, three-dimensional to them in a way we have largely lost, however much we have refined our "appreciation" of its visual beauty and increased our "respect for the environment." They were at least in no danger of abstracting themselves totally from their surroundings or divorcing themselves from their fellow creatures, even if their formal creeds might seem to preach that dogma. They felt contained by something larger than themselves and shared a deep sense of earnestness with the things they hooked and netted and shot, whereas we, no longer contained by a hostile wilderness, see no reason to contain ourselves. In this sense, the hunter is still infinitely preferable to the developer.

From their containment, their necessary contact with life around them, the old Cape Codders gained an intimate folk knowledge of the plants and animals they used, a knowledge expressed in the wonderful array of colloquial names that have almost entirely disappeared from common usage. Their world was full of pink-winks and pinkletinks, sawbellies and walleyes, timberdoodles and thistlebirds, dead-limb birds and fly-up-the-creeks, quawks and sea swallows, thunderpumpers and bog-suckers, peep-los, tee-os, and feebles—names that reflect a full range of sense knowledge, genuine affection, and a casual intimacy with wild creatures that can only be called a feeling of being at home.

From this same long and deep association grew what we call local folk crafts, the native products of a region whose hallmark, long before Frank Lloyd Wright, was the marriage of form and function. The traditional Cape Cod house, the dory, the catboat, the quahog rake, the cranberry scoop, and a hundred other structures and implements all possess a grace of shape and line, a fitness to purpose or task, which stems from an ingrained feeling for how they would fit into the wind, the tides, or the earth's greening bogs. Some of these crafts eventually flowered into art. During the early part of this century Elmer Crowell of Harwich traced the contours of ducks and shorebirds in blocks of pine and basswood with such skill and imagination that under his hands the craft of decoy-making was transformed into the art of bird-carving.

. . .

Today the culture of the old, isolated peninsula is gone, and with it the long compulsory associations with the land that bred it. Once freed from the necessity of direct physical contact, most men chose to remove themselves, almost in revulsion, from the scene. Only in the case of the local fisherman has the natural context of his work remained so awesome and encompassing that the presence and effect of the sea on human character have continued to outweigh its purely material yield. Probably no other occupation continues to exert such a strong and impractical hold on its participants.

Still, the majority of us, even those of us who profess to love the land and its history, would not wish to return to that earlier mode of life, even if we could. We have come back to the land with new eyes, new hands, new tools, and new perceptions. We have today much greater capacities for exploiting and understanding it, but the old choices remain.

Most of us choose to return in a highly selective and visually oriented manner, for recreation or for views. The contemporary land dealer offers us not a living but a "vista," and vistas are by common definition "distant views seen through a passage, as between buildings or rows of trees; scenes, prospects." We practice purely visual, or at best anticipatory, connections with the landscape, brief stops or glances at some pleasing prospect in our swift passages between resorts, homes, jobs, or marriages.

But there is another definition for the word, one that means "a comprehensive awareness of a series of remembered, present or anticipated events." Though a less common usage, it seems to capture the essence of that older, more intimate relationship to the land, whose inhabitants were so deeply involved in the natural life of their localities that every scene, every spot, every piece of earth and water offered not only a potential living but a vivid matrix of memory and anticipation.

Today we lack the source, and hence the feeling, of seasonal ritual that gave to our ancestors that "comprehensive awareness" of living in nature simultaneously in the past, present, and future. Our conscious need for nature is superficial and selective now. Our desire for ritual has been internalized into such expressions of our inner lives as football games, corporate retirements, and political conventions. Revivals of community festivals, which have become so popular in recent years, spring up hopefully, but tend to wither or become rather sad and forced affairs after a year or two, for the joy and earnestness they originated in, the celebrations of natural cycles of crop harvests, fish migrations, and animal births, are no longer there.

Our technology and economic leisure ought to allow us to reenter our environment with our full senses, to rediscover on a new plane of awareness and freedom what we have left behind. It would surely be a most prodigal return. There is, however, a deep reluctance in most people, largely unconfronted, to reenter the natural world, to "get back to nature" in any meaningful sense, despite the crowding of our beaches and the lip service paid to "ecology" and "the wonders of nature." We still prefer our nature packaged and safe, on our terms and time schedules, which of course is not nature at all. Perhaps we still sense it, unconsciously, as the source of too much pain and confinement, something struggled out of at too great a cost to court lightly again, still a threatening potential trap for the human spirit. Even now I find something ambivalent in my own feelings, especially when I am drawn most strongly toward nature, a reluctance to give myself entirely that withholds me and keeps me from pulling off to the side of the road and disappearing into the fields. It still seems too overwhelming, too cold, too real for human sensibilities. And yet we must make those first tentative steps, entering and remembering again, until we again become acclimated to the feel of it.

My aim in living where I do—on Cape Cod in the last quarter of the twentieth century—has been to try to reestablish this kind of close, tactile relationship to the landscape. I do not live in a traditional Cape Cod house, nor do I practice subsistence farming or fishing. As a child of technology I use its products, from cars to binoculars, to get me where I want to go and see what I want to see. And yet one of the primary reasons this place yields so much to me so consistently is that I have invested so much of myself into it, physically, mentally, and emotionally. I have cultivated its landscape as others have cultivated their gardens, sowing thoughts and expectations into its rich, sandy soil. It has been both my recreation and my study, my work and my play, so that when I look at a marsh, a wooded hillside, a kettle hole, a curve of beach, I receive back more than I would elsewhere because I not only know what these things look like but what they feel like, having established patterns of motion, rhythms of my own life in relationship to them.

I know what it is to work my way gingerly across a treacherous, pitted swath of salt hay on a marsh in early spring; to wade through the muck of a dark bog collecting frog's eggs in March; to hunker in the grass of an old field in April listening for woodcocks, or in October to watch milkweed seeds scatter in the wind; to feel the life shiver out of a herring as I hold its cold, slippery form and crack its head with a hammer for my corn patch; to float and yield myself to the thick, fertile waters of out-running tidal creeks in August; to rake for quahogs on a choppy September tide out on the long flats; to walk along the unstable, rounded erratics that comprise our stone walls or battle my way down through the jungles of catbrier and viburnum to the bottom of a kettle hole; to pull oars against a spraying autumn wind in the middle of Pleasant Bay, or sway from the top of a resin-soaked white pine above a sea of ruddy oaks; to place warm shingles on a roof on a perfect October day, or run berserk among a congregation of a thousand sedate gulls on a sandy plain in January; to split blocks of oak in April, cut from my neighbor's woods in November, that will feed my stove next February; to feel the spray of breakers from a northeaster on the Outer Beach; to walk along the hard, frozen wrack line of the beach in winter, or across its soft, popping summer sands.

These and a thousand other simple physical acts have given this particular landscape a richness for me so that even its most casual aspect is filled, not with slick charm or abstract nostalgia, but present, living tactile memory.

My hands yearn to know them, all the forms of this land, to add depth and texture to my eyes. Touch, knowledgeable and earnest, adds so much to vision that it, and not hearing, is the natural accompaniment in the shaping of human experience. Hand and eye are the makers of man; they need one another for whole being, whole thought. Even now, as I write, my eyes guide my hand as it tries to render back what touch once revealed to sight.

Nighttracking

THE SECOND SNOW began about nine in the evening. The first had fallen the night before, all night long like soft white feathers, and by morning there were nearly eight inches of it on the ground. In places in the woods it was over a foot deep, much of it fallen from the limbs above. For a short while we were in Vermont.

By noon the wind had picked up from the northwest, ripping the carefully raised ridges from the branches and slinging them against the trunks, where they exploded like soft, silent bombs. Sharp gusts churned the deep kettle hole below the house into a whirling cauldron of mist and snow, sending suspended streams of snow dust sailing wraithlike into the woods.

Late in the afternoon the lean oaks raised their long branches skyward, like the gaunt arms of starved desire. Their long blue shadows reached out across the white yard, swaying and crossing in the wind like swords; the blurred tips passed through the glass doors and onto the throw rug, nipping at my toes. A solitary hawk sailed and banked, burning against the snow-rose ridge to the south.

This evening's snow was different, beginning earlier and falling in tiny, fast, hard flakes. I had planned to go to bed early, but its steady persistence tempted me out for a late walk. I started up my neighbor's drive, an old wood road that slowly winds its way up the southern flank of Dry Hill. There were footprints and tracks where she had been out earlier in the evening with her dogs, but these were already blurred and filling in with the new snow.

The moon remained invisible, but its diffuse gibbous light dimly illuminated the road before me. The night air was filled with tiny blue glints of light, like blue fireflies in a winter's night garden. I switched on my flashlight briefly and looked for signs of life abroad—deer, mouse, or skunk—but no other tracks were visible in the accumulating snow. All things were hidden away; even the owls were silent. I became aware of the sound of individual flakes ticking against my coat, a gentle collective seethe among the dark branches, and farther off, a soft textured wind, too distant to matter.

The snow was all there was. It fell with a gentle, steady falling, an unhurried persistence that seemed more inexhaustible than the wildest blinding blizzard. The larger pine boughs hung heavily down, clotted with snow, not cracked or bent, but pressed as by the concentrated weight of countless soft, insistent fingers. The smaller understory spruces drooped like half-closed umbrellas, a few branches sticking out oddly like Chinese characters twisting in the wind.

Near the top of the drive I left my neighbor's tracks and veered off onto a footpath that gradually descended through the woods down to the town road. Here the snow was unbroken, and the path became only a dim band of lesser darkness winding through the crooked labyrinth of trunks. Almost immediately I bumped against a tall young sapling. Its long, spindly limbs reared above me, a wild net of twigs and branches. For a moment I was gripped by a childish fear of the grotesque, and stepped aside.

Snapping my light on, I continued, more cautiously, along the path. About halfway down the hill several sets of deer tracks crossed the path, heading south, away from the house. The tracks seemed fairly fresh, and though the snow was deep and still falling, I could make out the clear split-pear imprint of a hoof at the bottom of each narrow white well. I had never tracked an animal at night before, but this seemed a clear invitation, and I left the path, following the prints with the beam of my flashlight into the dark woods.

There were at least two, maybe three different sets of tracks—it was hard to tell. They would come together, then part for a few yards, then come together again. Sometimes one would go off to one side for a few false steps and, after hesitating, return again to the main track. They followed no obvious game trails, however, and were not easy to keep up with, for I had to keep my beam pointing downward at the tracks and yet negotiate the underbrush and watch out for low limbs.

I have always been fascinated that animals as large as deer can move so quietly through heavy underbrush, but now I was amazed at where these tracks seemed to go. Without breaking stride or even disturbing the snow above them, they dipped beneath thick overhanging branches and deadfalls less than three feet off the ground. Several times I nearly lost the tracks when I had to circle around some obstruction they had passed easily beneath. At other times there seemed to be no passage at all for them ahead, and yet the tracks sailed smoothly through, like real prints left by phantom deer.

Nonetheless, the tracks soon appeared to get quite fresh. I sensed I was very near my quarry, that at any moment I might turn and brush up against a warm, soft flank. But though I pitched the light over and over out into the darkness, all I saw were bare oak branches, limned with snow like the bleached interlocked antlers of stags. Once I thought I heard a sound behind me, and once I caught a glimpse of shining yellow eyes off low in the woods.

It was clear they were now aware of my presence, even if I could not see them. The tracks began to take on a more erratic, evasive pattern. They seemed to double back, making frequent sharp turns. Occasionally there were startling leaps, hiatuses in the snow, of nearly ten feet, so that again I nearly lost them several times. Then I realized they were deliberately circling, that I was crossing and recrossing not only the same deer tracks, but my own as well.

I now had no idea where I was, nor how long I had been following the deer tracks. It might have been ten minutes, or forty. And yet I continued to pursue them, burrowing after them with my light like a mole in the night, trusting the light and the tracks to lead me eventually back to the path. The snow had begun to fall more heavily, thickening the darkness. It occurred to me, in some corner of my brain, that if the batteries failed, I might wander in these woods for hours, unseen and unheard. There were no streetlights, no houselights on, no stars to steer by, and though I knew the road could not be far away, it was unlikely any cars would pass by this late at night.

Perhaps it was melodramatic to think I was in any real danger, perhaps not. At any rate I did not stop to consider it, for I was hooked by my quest, dragged like a whaler on a Nantucket sleighride. This was not the first time I have been seduced by the gentle character of the Cape landscape into a reckless cutting loose of my moorings. I have at times felt contempt for those summer bathers and boaters who have no respect for the strength and violence of the ocean they play in, but here, in these dark woods, I was really no better.

I stopped, stood up straight, and switched off the light in a conscious effort to break the spell of pursuit. I saw nothing, heard nothing but the empty soughing of wind through the pines. I felt the tiny silver flakes glancing against my cheeks. My hot breath had congealed in miniature icy bells on the tips of my moustache. I felt them with my tongue, and the cold, clear, hard touch seemed to bring me back to myself.

All at once the tracking seemed pointless, if it had ever had a point. I knew I had not ever really expected to catch up with the deer, but only hoped to feel their nearness, to sense their passage in the night. Now what I sensed around me was a silent, annoyed indifference, which, I sometimes think, is the attitude of wild animals toward men when we disturb them, and even when we destroy them.

It had really been the snow, not the tracks, that led me on—the silent, obliterating snow, like a white sea on which I had set out unawares. There is something about snow, something about the way it erases backgrounds and covers up old connections and lines of obligation, the way each tree and rock and figure stands out against it, separate and enormously palpable, that tempts us into letting go our bearings, slipping our short leashes of security for the sake of promised encounters and new meetings in the dark.

But something had broken the spell, some saving sense of absurdity, perhaps. A few moments later I stumbled upon one of my neighbor's boundary markers, a steel tube with a large *H* marked in the top of its concrete marrow. Suddenly, as though spoken to, I knew where I was—less than two hundred feet, as it turned out, from the road.

A Swallow Summer

O N   T H E   B E A C H facing Cape Cod Bay, not far
from where I live, there is a large outcropping of
blue clay. It is perhaps 125 feet long, beginning in some
low sand dunes at either end and rising to a height of
about 15 feet in the middle. Above the clay is another 4
feet or so of gravelly outwash till, surmounted by a thin
layer of drift sand. The crest is heavily vegetated with
beach plum, bayberry, and poison ivy. During the past
few years the outcropping has undergone severe and
unusually rapid erosion, resulting in nearly vertical walls
of clay and a thick fringe of exposed roots and overhanging branches at the top.

This past spring a colony of bank swallows took up
residence in this clay outcrop. The bank swallow, or
sand martin, is a fairly uncommon nester on the Cape,
much less numerous than the tree swallows and barn
swallows one commonly sees flitting and veering over the
salt marshes in swift pursuit of insects. Bank swallows
are colonial nesters that dig burrows in sand or gravel
banks, usually along watercourses. They are most com-

mon in glaciated sections of the country, but breed widely from Maine to California and from Alaska to Texas.

These birds are extraordinarily site-tenacious, and some swallow colonies are quite old. There is a famous colony in the ocean cliffs at North Truro, for instance, which Thoreau observed during his visit to the Highland Lighthouse in June of 1850. Though the cliffs have eroded several hundred feet since then and the colony's numbers have fluctuated drastically in the interim, the birds are still there—an occupation whose length, in generations, exceeds that of the Hopi cliff dwellers.

Because the banks these swallows nest in are the result of natural erosion or human excavation, their situation is always somewhat precarious. River floods, ocean storms, sand avalanches, and pit digging are all potential threats to their chosen habitat. Despite this, the bank swallow is the only swallow that does not nest in human structures. As Edward Howe Forbush put it, "It prefers to dig its own hole." Indeed, its stubborn preference for nesting sites is reflected even in its scientific name, *Riparia riparia riparia* ("Bank, bank, bank").

Bank swallows have been known to arrive on the Cape as early as April 30, though they do not normally show up in numbers until the second week in May. Unlike many of our upland birds, the swallows arrive on the coast earlier than they do on the mainland, gradually following the estuaries and rivers inland and dispersing over the countryside. Forbush observed that when they arrive at a former colony site, they will sleep in the old holes, or, if there are none, will immediately excavate new ones.

Spring storms present a major threat to such early-arriving birds. If there are not enough holes, many birds will seek shelter in a single burrow, sometimes pinning each other to death. If sand plugs up a hole in which they have taken refuge, they may be unable to dig themselves out and so be buried alive. The bay beach colony that I found this spring was a new one, however. I first noticed it during the last week in May, when a dozen or more birds were busy excavating in the sandy upper layers of the cliff, and over twenty holes had been begun or completed.

During the weekend of June 11–13, an unusually late and intense southeast blow scoured our peninsula, dumping four inches of rain and keeping temperatures in the low fifties for several days on end, turning our young tomato plants a sickly yellow. Fortunately for the swallows, and also for their human neighbors, the storm occurred during a period of neap tides, so that the beaches suffered no further erosion. The colony's north-northwest exposure and overhanging veil of roots and branches probably helped to protect it from the driving sand as well. But prolonged cold rains can be just as deadly to these insect-eaters. At such times, Forbush writes, "The poor birds then huddle together in their holes, and being unable to find food, they perish."

During the bad weather, however, the swallows must somehow have managed to find food, or else were just tough enough to stick it out. When the sun finally re-emerged and I went back to revisit the colony, I found it more healthy and thriving than ever, busy and bustling, with nearly sixty holes now pitting the top few feet of sand and clay banking.

Several of the birds were chasing insects just outside the holes with their quick, crooked, batlike flight, so that it was difficult at first to get a bead on any of them. Occasionally one would dart into a burrow without ceremony and emerge a few seconds later just as quickly, swooping down several feet as it came out and then rising, in a manner reminiscent of the way murres and gannets take off from their seaside breeding cliffs.

After several minutes, I finally spotted one peering out from the entrance to its burrow. Focusing my binoculars on it, I could see clearly its distinguishing dark throat band, with a little ragged dart hanging down from the middle. The throat patch above was a creamy white, but the breast below appeared somewhat muddy or soiled, perhaps a result of excavation work in its burrow. Although its small head jerked about continually, the bird had a settled look about it, as though it had made a commitment. The swallows were apparently here to stay, and I was determined to get to know them.

It was not until June 20 that I returned to the bank swallow colony for my first close look at these birds. By then the bay beach was hot, and the human summer was also in full swing. Several dozen people had spread out on the town beach and spilled over onto the area in front of the clay banking. Most were sitting on blankets and towels, leaning back on their palms and facing the water, unaware of the swallows darting in and out of the holes above their heads. I spread my towel between two of the sunbathers, sat down facing the cliff, and stared upward into a bright, hurting haze.

The sixty or so holes in the colony had all been dug in the band of gravelly sand that sat atop the clay ledges and spread out over one hundred feet along the bank. They had been placed in three loose but distinct levels, one to four feet below the crest, though most were in the lower level. Near the right end of the colony was a single, larger hole over five inches in diameter, the burrow of the kingfisher that I had heard rattling around the colony when I first visited it in late May.

Several of the birds were perched at the hole entrances, uttering a continuous stream of buzzing, querulous noises back and forth, like the low, perfunctory talk of construction crews on a coffee break. Bird books describe bank swallows as having brown backs, but these appeared more a soft slate gray. They are the smallest of our swallows, yet as well fashioned as any for the tasks to which they were born.

Even more of the swallows were perched on the veil of roots and branches that hung down from the eroded crest in front of their burrows, engaged, it seemed, in outdoor socializing. One pair sat face to face on a root, about six inches apart, constantly preening and softly buzzing for nearly ten minutes on end. Their wings were beautifully swept back, giving them, like terns, the impression of motion while at rest. Like terns also, they are restless, aggressive, and highly nervous. I felt that any activity that held such mercurial birds in one position for so long must have a more than casual purpose to it. In fact the tête-à-tête preening had a kind of ritualistic quality, part of a constant tension and innate hostility all colonial nesters seem to contend with.

Perhaps, I fancied, they were just congratulating one another on their choice of site, which was a fine one. The vertical clay bank provided a solid underfooting for the burrows and a deterrent to human climbers. The sand layer above was easy to dig in, and the heavily vegetated overhanging crest presented a barrier to predators from above and convenient perches near the holes. In addition there was an area of dune grass and brackish marsh just around the corner from the colony where the birds could conveniently obtain insect food for themselves and their young all summer long.

Altogether it must have seemed "just the spot" for these birds, a nice family resort hotel with a shopping center within easy flying distance. The swallows seemed to share a sense of satisfaction with the sunbathers below them. Erosion to them was not a destroyer but a maker of home-sites, as it is also a maker of summer beaches. Both groups were, in a sense, benefiting from destruction. The difference, I suppose, was that the swallows had no expectations about what the place, or life itself, owed them.

The following day I returned again to the swallow colony. The weather had turned cool and clouded, the tide was out, and the birds and I had the beach to ourselves.

If the day before had presented a scene of reassuring domesticity, this afternoon was all squabbling pugnaciousness. The air was full of packs of two, three, and four birds, chasing one another with fierce buzzings, then suddenly scattering and darting out over the flats. One scrapping group included two birds and a large mourning cloak butterfly that acted more like a participant than an object of prey.

On the other hand, these small and constant dogfights were balanced by long, leisurely flights taken by individual pairs. These did not seem to be food-gathering flights, for they involved long, smooth glides during which the birds stayed together, slipping back and forth across one another, in a manner very similar to the courtship flight of terns.

It seems, in fact, quite difficult to distinguish aggression and affection, work and play, in these birds. One writer, for instance, claims that "Bank swallows seem to take the work of excavating their burrows very lightly, more like play than work." They did take frequent "flight breaks" from their digging, as though it were too sedentary a task for these restless creatures to stay at very long at a stretch. When the birds gather feathers with which to line their burrows, they sometimes engage in "feather play," passing the feathers from bird to bird and tossing them into the air.

Despite such frivolities and mock fighting, there was still a good deal of serious excavation going on at that late date. One bird I watched was just beginning a new hole about two and a half feet down from the top of the bank. At first it gripped the face of the slope with its claws, using its tail as a brace, woodpecker fashion, and pecking away at the sandy wall with its small beak. As it got farther in, it began to use its feet as well, which presumably became the primary digging tools as it progressed. Bank swallows are said to dig at a rate of three to four inches a day, and have been known to mine tunnels nine feet long.

Even when they are working, there is a great deal of jockeying and adjusting going on among the members of a colony. As the bird I watched pursued its digging, another one flew up and landed on the lip of another hole about eight inches to its right. The first bird immediately jumped across to the second and chased it away. Then it jumped down to another hole eighteen inches lower where a third swallow was perched. This one it did not chase off, but visited with briefly, buzzing and twirping, before leaping back up to its original hole and resuming work.

The roughly equidistant spacing of the holes (eight to

eighteen inches apart) suggested possible limits to each male's territory, though perhaps structural as well as territorial considerations were involved. Moreover, "territory" has a complex and shifting meaning when applied to these colonial nesters. Apparently a great deal of communal digging can be involved. Male and female ordinarily work together in excavating a burrow, but up to six swallows have been known to work on a single hole and then move on together to the next one. Burrows are occasionally shared by more than one pair for breeding, and there are reports of orphaned chicks having been fed by adults in adjacent holes.

All of these traits distinguish a bank swallow "community" from a mere colony of close-nesting species such as gulls and gannets, where not only is there no cooperation between pairs in nest building or chick raising, but territories are jealously guarded to the point where a wandering chick may have its skull crushed by the beak of a neighboring parent whose domain it has inadvertently invaded.

Despite these remarkable instances of swallow cooperation, however, the mock fights and chases I observed that day still seemed an outlet for very real tension and aggression. The holes were used by the swallows as frequently to escape other birds pursuing them as for any other purpose, and the whole hillside emanated a constant buzzing, like static electricity.

I asked myself, What is the use of all this squabbling and bickering? Yet later it seemed that there had been a kind of communal amorousness to it all, a need of being both together and apart with which I could identify. It expressed a tension whose conflicts were resolved, or at least kept in dynamic balance, by a matrix of mock fights, chases, paired flights, preenings, and countless other maneuvers and tactics that I could not hope to catch in one afternoon's watching. Perhaps the connection I felt was that each bird had its own pressing individual needs which it somehow managed to gratify within the strictures of the community.

I did not return again until July 10. When I arrived on the beach it was close to sunset; the late, intense light shone over the bay and coated the eroded cliffs with a certain stark and ageless grandeur, like that of ancient Palestinian walls. Recent rains had washed over the protruding clay ledges, creating cavelike sculpture, quick and temporary tapestries, and stalactites.

There was still no sign of young at the burrows' entrances, nor did I ever see any; but my visits had been so scattered and superficial that it was likely many had already fledged. Most of the swallows that evening were flying over the dune area and brackish marsh just west of the colony. I had read that after the young no longer require brooding, the parents cease to sleep in the burrows with them and roost separately with the other adults in nearby marshes.

Against a summer sunset stuffed with clouds they swung silently and wheeled with easy grace over the rising grasses, reaping invisible gnats, flies, mosquitoes, and other insects. Swallows are the diurnal counterparts of bats, and like the bat's crooked flight, their constant veering and banking are determined by the prey they follow. There has been sufficient praise for the hawk's eye and soaring flight, for the owl's ear and silent pounce, for the poetry of geese and the grace of terns. But for sheer aerial competence, nothing surpasses these swallows on the wing.

My last visit to the swallow colony was on August 16. All but a few of the birds had left the site, and those that remained had not entered the burrows for over a week; so I decided to investigate these nesting cavities.

I arrived early in the morning at the clay outcrop on the beach, but found that I had been preceded. During the past couple of weeks the clay faces of the cliffs had been discovered by some of the younger summer visitors, and now carved testimonies of adolescent love (presumably representing something more enduring than love letters in the sand) adorned their smooth vertical faces. That morning a teenaged boy was already industriously at work when I arrived, creating an unusually elaborate version of his girlfriend's name with foot-high letters etched in relief on the earthen walls. He had even carved a little ledge in which to place his transistor radio while he worked.

Not wanting to disturb the young artist, I walked out on the flats for a while. When he had finished and left, I returned and climbed up onto the clay ledges, from which all but the uppermost of the nesting cavities were accessible. Of the sixty holes I had counted from the beach, most appeared to be false starts, only a few inches deep, where the bank swallows had encountered large stones or had abandoned the digging for some other reason.

I measured twenty burrows that appeared deep enough to have contained nests. These had an average depth of fourteen and one-half inches and a maximum depth of thirty-seven inches. Almost all sloped slightly upward as they went in, a measure designed to keep the burrows well drained.

Eight of the deeper holes contained evidence of active nesting: grass, feathers, egg remnants, or large flea populations. But one intact nest that I found surprised me. It had been constructed in a mere scrape in the cliff and projected halfway out over the edge. Near it I found where two others had obviously been placed in similar positions but had fallen out and lay partway down the slope. This suggested that bank swallow nests are not always placed deep inside a burrow but are sometimes built right on the lip of ledges, much as cliff swallow nests are. Perhaps, then, many of the shallow holes that I had considered false starts were also the sites of nests that had fallen out, and the total number of nests was greater than the remaining evidence indicated.

I took home three of the still-intact nests to examine more closely. All were of the same basic size and structure: round, flattened bowls about five inches across and one and one-half inches high at the sides. The bases were carefully and tightly woven of eelgrass strands and pieces of marsh hay, but the bowls were copiously lined with the creamy-white breast feathers of gulls, which must have been in abundant supply for the swallows on the flats. In one of the nests there remained two unhatched eggs, elliptical in shape and about three-quarters of an inch long. They were white with small black flecks, though the flecks were not pigment but extraneous material that scraped off. Considering the size of both the eggs and the birds, they were fairly large nests, and extremely comfortable ones.

The swallows were gone. Their empty nesting holes, at whose entrances they had darted like bright, gray pupils, now stared out blindly. They had been here for a brief summer, and whether they would return next year was more uncertain than with most bird species, for their cliff home would be subject to a winter of tide and storm, of shifting bars and currents, of fickle winds and the unpredictable effects of man-made structures—vagaries and afflictions which would also erode the emblems of summer romance that now decorated their clay walls.

The fact that I had seen as much as I did in my few cursory visits to the colony suggested how much more went unobserved. I owed these small swallows more attention than I had given them, but the shoreline has always contained more lives than any one man can trace in his lifetime. I had first been attracted to the birds as a kind of curiosity, and had stayed long enough to catch glimpses of a complex mutual life that was more than mere "colonial" nesting. The swallow community is another expression of the social principle of nature, in many ways tuggingly suggestive of our own, though fundamentally distinct from and foreign to it. I was not equipped or trained to follow its development objectively, and though I was free to draw what analogies I might, I knew they would illuminate my own life more than the birds'.

In their comings and goings there had been expressions of the ambiguities of love and aggression, work and play, individuality and group action that all communities struggle with. Like us, they are premier opportunists, using both what the ocean throws up and what it tears away. One could not blame them, in fact, if they, too, sometimes felt that the mighty processes of shore and sea had been created for their benefit alone.

The Seals of Jeremy Point

THE EXTREMES OF Cape Cod's land mass are
horizontal rather than vertical, our outermost points
the ends of sandspits instead of the peaks of mountains.
Whether formed by wind and wave or the earth's internal
upthrusts, however, the nature of both extremes is
ultimate exposure, stratospheric or oceanic. The whole
curving peninsula, for that matter, is a rising horizontal
Matterhorn, a flattened precipice projecting outward
rather than upward, but an imposing eminence nonetheless, full of isolated grandeur.

One of the outermost of these outermost reaches is
Jeremy Point in Wellfleet. Jeremy Point is the broadened
tip of a long sandspit that stretches south from Great
Beach Hill. It is the last link in a seven-mile stretch of
tombolos, a series of barrier beaches connecting several
islands to the mainland and forming the elongated western border of Wellfleet Harbor.

The islands, in this case, are bold, rounded hills of
glacial drift and were once real islands, as most of their
names—Bound Brook Island, Griffin Island, Great Island

—suggest. But over the centuries the rising sea level in Cape Cod Bay has eaten away at their western flanks, creating steep marine scarps and connecting them with thin sandy barrier beaches backed by dunes and salt marsh systems.

This, at least, is the accepted geological history of these islands, though on one of his journeys to the Cape, Thoreau made the puzzling and tantalizing comment that "These harbor islands of Wellfleet were said to have been connected during the last century, and may be so again."

I had been out to Great Island several times on foot, and once or twice as far as Great Beach Hill. But the first time I ever walked the entire length of the tombolos to Jeremy Point was one day last winter, and the reason was seals.

Over the past decade herds of northern harbor seals have increasingly congregated, or "hauled out," on the Cape's more isolated beaches and islands at low tide during the winter months. One of the largest herds winters at Jeremy Point. Only the week before, from the bluffs across the harbor, I had looked through binoculars and seen a number of low, long dark forms scattered on the Point, though it was hard to tell from that distance whether they were seals or chunks of ice.

So, one sunny, windy morning in early February, I parked the car at the National Seashore's lot on Griffin Island and set off across the Gut, a barrier beach connecting Griffin with Great Island. Cape Cod Bay had not yet frozen over, though the marshes and coves on the harbor side were well glazed with sheets of salt ice. Groups of brant fed on both sides of the Gut, and scattered clumps of oysters lined the beach above the ice, probably dropped by gulls. I gathered a pocketful of the unfrozen ones to take home with me later.

I walked down the inner side of Great Island, keeping to the shore. Just above the marsh grass was the beached and devastated carcass of an eight-foot tuna, an imposing fish with a large head, a thick body, and small, sharp teeth, lying at right angles to the tide.

On the hillside above me the winter vegetation of the Cape spread in subtle and impressive variation: low green and wine-colored mats of bearberry; bright, textured, lime-colored shags of reindeer lichen interspersed with black splotches of dead plants; gray rags and cushions of poverty grass; bare blue-gray scrub oak bushes in the shallow hollows, with last year's leaves lying like copper plates around their bases; dark-green brushes of young pitch pines; and the tawny, bleached stands of beach grass, bent stiffly over in the wind.

I walked diagonally on the marked path up the hillside and into the pine woods above. These are some of the premier pine barrens of the Cape, a gentle and inviting woods, yet with a strangely desolate and blasted look from inside. Beneath their shade long, wheat-colored grass spreads out like a soft carpet. The ground is littered with dead and dying pine trunks, gray and crumbling, the victims of frequent blowdowns rather than fire. Many of the trunks of living trees are curiously cracked open several feet above their bases. The heartwood of these pines frequently rots out until the trunks are unable to bear their weight and crack outward around the entire circumference like Chinese lanterns, or as though firecrackers had been exploded inside them. They may go on living in this precarious way for years with the wind and the sun shining through their slotted sides.

I came after a short distance to the Smith Tavern site, a cleared space of jumbled cobblestones marked with a simple plaque: "Great Island Whaler's Tavern (1690–1740)."

A Seashore trail leaflet, picked up at the parking lot, told me that a sign to the tavern once stood on the beach. It was long gone, of course, but the words have survived the centuries as a local ditty:

> *Samuel Smith, he has good flip,*
> *Good toddy, if you please,*
> *The way is near and very clear,*
> *'Tis just beyond the trees.*

Though these islands were entirely deforested when Thoreau viewed Wellfleet Harbor in the 1850s, tree-planting programs and natural reclamation have made these lines appropriate again.

There were several pictures on wooden stands, one showing the outline of the building's unusually large square foundation, another of various artifacts found during the Seashore's excavation of the site in the 1960s: pewter spoons, clay pipes, pieces of red earthenware, lead windowpanes, bits of glass and ladies' fans, wrought-iron hardware, pieces of whalebone, brass finials, a harpoon, a 1724 farthing.

Fragments of an English world transplanted to a land not yet far from wilderness. Fragments of a world long gone, amid which I now stood trying to remember and re-create it across a clearing of scattered stones, even as the earth remembers and re-creates itself, reclaiming, reestablishing its original communities through the slow process of tree succession and the gradual return of deer, owls, ospreys, terrapins, and—so I hoped to find—seals.

Passing through these woods, I came out on the top of a steep eroding bluff on the southeast side of the island

and made my way down to the beach through a cut. Slipping off my pack, I sat down and looked out at the harbor before me. It was a peaceful scene, serene and temperate here in the lee of the island. Gulls and sanderlings picked at their ease on the glistening flats, while brant paddled quietly in the water farther out. The sandbank above me gathered warmth from the bright morning sun. The temperature where I sat must have been in the high forties. I took off my hat, parka, and gloves, loosened my wool shirt, and basked in the sun.

Less than a half-mile to the west, on the Bay side of the island, the air temperature was about twenty-five degrees, with a cutting northwest wind whose wind chill factor likely brought the effective temperature well below zero. Thus there was a relative differential of some fifty degrees from one side of the island to the other. As I said, our extremes are horizontal.

It was almost noon before I finally stood at the southern end of Great Beach Hill, the last island in the tombolo chain. A small wooden sign stuck in the sand said that I had come 3 miles from the parking lot on Griffin Island and that it was another 1.2 miles to Jeremy Point.

I might have found this information more encouraging if I had not learned, from experience, that distances on the Cape's outer fringes are approximate at best, often misleading, and never the same for very long. Even if the figures were accurate, there were other factors. My hike had thus far been clothed by the forests and bluffs of the islands, with only short streaks across the naked stretches of the connecting barrier beaches. The last part, however, would be almost totally exposed, with a thirty-knot, subfreezing wind quartering across my starboard stern.

I looked down the long, narrow sandspit stretching toward Jeremy Point. The spit seemed to become very thin and was apparently covered at times by high tides, for sections of the sand were capped with large chunks of broken ice. I set out with a sharp wind blowing at my back, freezing my right ear despite my woolen cap. I might regret it coming back, but for the moment the sand was firm, the wind was with me, and I was buoyed along by visions of sunbathing seals.

It was slow going over the salt ice, but after another half-hour of sliding and slipping along, I reached Jeremy Point. It consisted of a couple of steep sand wedges, each about ten feet high and sharply eroded on the Bay side, and was in fact—as the Seashore sign had said and as my USGS map indicated—a little over a mile south of Great Beach Hill. What neither sign nor map had told me, however, was that since the map was printed in 1958, an extension of the spit had built up, curving and hooking away at least another half-mile to the southeast.

Discouraged, I slumped in the shelter of the larger of the two dunes. More salt ice obscured the end of the new spit so that I still could not tell whether there were any seals hauled out on its tip. My right foot had begun to hurt, and I knew that every yard farther on would be an additional yard and a half coming back with the wind full in my face.

But the winter sun, noon-high and bright, seemed to lead me on. I left my small pack at the base of the dune and followed on down a wagging, wavering, ragged tail of sand and ice, in a landscape that grew progressively more abstract and surreal. Now all vegetation or hope of vegetation had disappeared. The harbor flats were left behind and the deeper water, nearly at ebb, crowded around both sides of the ice-edged spit.

All the way down from Great Island I had followed a thinning procession of tracks—cat, dog, human, gull— made ahead of me in the sands during periods of thaw. By the time I reached Jeremy Point, only the gull tracks were left, and now even these had disappeared. For life, I had only the company of some offshore eiders, rocking in the dark waters with their long, horselike bills.

Several hundred yards offshore to the southwest were the remains of Billingsgate Island, the Cape's Atlantis, a thriving fishing community during the nineteenth century that disappeared beneath the waves during the early decades of this one. The remains, visible only at low tide, were surprisingly impressive: not just anonymous shoals, but piles of large rocks, the ruins of lost foundations of homes, schoolhouses, and a lighthouse. Seen in brilliant silhouette, they looked more like prehistoric ruins than the fairly modern rubble they were, an impression which added to the sense of the relativity of time out here on such a geological limb.

Along this last stretch of sandspit I happened upon one of those incongruous objects sometimes thrown up by the tide: a large, heavy wooden rolling pin which, except for one handle broken off, was in excellent shape. I picked it up and carried it along with me, though I suppose I might have safely left it to retrieve on the way back.

At the very end of the spit the tip widened out slightly, rose into a low mound, and became heavily encrusted with stranded ice floes. I approached it with a sense of completing an arduous and somewhat unsatisfying obligation and was about to come up over the last rise when one of the pale ice slabs suddenly moved and rolled over, revealing the darker, spotted back of a large harbor seal.

There were six or seven of them visible at the crest of the mound, just beyond the ice, where the beach began to slant down toward the water. They were all stretched out, basking lazily in the sun on the south-facing slope as though hauled out on some tropical beach. I hunched down quickly behind an ice mass to watch them. The larger ones appeared to be almost five feet long, though size is notoriously deceptive in places like this where there is nothing familiar to gauge it by.

I was no more than fifty feet from the seals, however. Most had pale, fish-colored bellies turned toward me, the hind flippers and short tails tucked against their bodies. They had apparently neither seen nor heard me approach, just as I had not noticed them, though they had the light and wind advantage. For a few moments, at least, I had that rare and marvelous privilege of observing at close range large, wild animals that were completely unaware of my presence.

One of them lazily turned its head and seemed to be looking directly at me. But either its air vision and smell were not very keen, or it simply did not see in my blue-capped head anything that constituted a threat. I tried to maintain a peaceful expression on my face, but it was hard to suppress the excitement generated by such wild nearness. They, in their turn, conveyed that sense of well-being of a pride of lions resting on an African veldt, yawning, scratching themselves and each other, rolling slowly and fatly over like the most vulgar of summer sunbathers. I was prepared to remain crouched watching them for some time, but another seal looked my way with its dark brown eyes, and this time it seemed to take notice. There was no doubt it was looking *at* me now, evaluating, deciding. And then it began slowly but deliberately humping its way down the beach to the water.

My cover blown, I leaped up and ran at them full tilt. The seals exploded into action. As I came up over the crest I saw at least sixty of them, all headed away from me toward the water. Some were already splashing in, others were rowing energetically across the sand with their front flippers, bouncing their fat but supple torsos down the beach, their useless tails and hind flippers tucked under.

Even with such frantic exertion, however, they could not make much more than five miles an hour on land, and it was easy for me to run around and cut off most of the herd a few yards from the water. Surprisingly, they did not stop, turn aside, or even slow down, but simply made a minimal detour around me.

I had the simultaneous impression of a school of dolphins and a pack of large dogs swarming around me. They were almost comic in their ungainly earnestness to reach the water, but when I reached down to touch a small three-foot seal as it passed within a foot of me, the animal opened its mouth, snarling and snorting, barking and feinting at me with sharp canine teeth. I lurched backward involuntarily and all at once was struck by the reality of the situation. Here I was, standing between a pack of agitated marine carnivores and an icy harbor, miles from the nearest human. Suppose they had all decided to be wolves instead of sheep? It is amazing how unconsciously we act on the reputation of animals, benign or otherwise, when an objective appraisal might radically alter our attitudes, as it did mine now. From that moment I stood absolutely still, but the seals were interested only in gaining the water and dashed past me, disappearing rapidly once they reached it.

After the last seal had passed by me I ventured to move again. I turned to see a host of round, whiskered heads bobbing in the water, fifty to a hundred feet from shore. Now they were the observers, peering at me with dark, hollow eyes. They dove noisily, thrashing their tails and spraying water as they went under, as though saying in defiance, "*Now* we are on equal footing!"

Sixty or more quasi-humanoid heads staring in your direction tend to promote self-consciousness in any situation. I walked back up the beach, past their fanned-out slipper prints and twisting body tracks, and came to where they had been basking only minutes before, an area of sand and ice covered with loose white droppings.

I went over the crest and crouched down behind the ice again for several minutes. When I lifted my head the seals had moved only a few yards closer to land, alerted now, perhaps, to my scent. So, giving them a farewell wave, I turned and made my way slowly back against the cutting wind across the sand, gravel, and slush ice of this tongue of wave-shaped "land."

It was only when I saw my shadow in front of me that I realized I had been carrying the rolling pin in my left hand throughout the whole episode. Had the seals noticed it? Had I perhaps instinctively lifted it when they charged? Had it influenced their behavior at all? Probably not, but I saw it now not merely as an interesting piece of beach flotsam, but a potential weapon or tool. It became something I might have used to defend myself with, or perhaps even to have bludgeoned the small one with to obtain life essentials, if that had been necessary.

At any rate, it gave to my hulking, limping, elongated shadow a primitive outline, suggesting possibilities I had not expected to contemplate. I seemed to have been walking along a beach more remote than I knew.

Summer Flats

As far as summer clamming goes, I am admittedly a winter snob. Normally I set foot on our tidal flats with bucket and rake only during the R months, plus May—not because I fear red tide or other health hazards during the hot weather, but because conditions are more to my liking in the off-season.

The quahog or hard-shell clam beds in our town are divided roughly into winter and summer flats. The former, located along the eastern half of our shoreline, are open for quahogging from October through May; the latter, in the western half, are open from June through September. For various environmental reasons, shellfish are much more plentiful on these eastern flats. Moreover, one can take them any day of the week that the temperature is above freezing; whereas on the western, or summer, flats, taking in July and August is limited to Sundays and Thursdays, which may not always coincide with the best tides or weather.

Quahogs on the winter flats are also more "wild." That is, though seedbeds are maintained by the shellfish department in this area, the abundance and distribution of adult quahogs is still primarily dependent on the un-regulated influences of Cape Cod Bay rather than on human manipulation. The summer flats, on the other hand, support no large, permanent shellfish populations and must be periodically stocked with adult quahogs during the summer months in order to ensure an adequate supply. Thus summer quahogging tends to be largely a "put and take" affair, designed primarily to make summer visitors feel that they have gotten their money's worth for their fifteen-dollar nonresident shellfish license and have participated in some authentic Cape Cod activity. I have no quarrel with this, since the price of their illusion helps to subsidize my own winter habit in the other half of town.

There are numerous other advantages to winter clamming—a scarcity of other clammers, the lack of insects, the presence of all sorts of waterfowl, searingly intense sunsets, and so on—but it would be tedious and perhaps cruel to enumerate them all, especially the smug satisfaction I get from knowing that certain high-priced waterfront condominiums that now line much of the shore where I rake in winter are owned almost entirely by summer residents who in July may, from their $200,000-and-up units, look out on but not touch the quahog beds where in January I may harvest ten quarts a week for the princely sum of five bucks. I told you I was a snob about this matter of winter clamming.

So it was with some reluctance, and purely out of friendship, that I agreed to take a visiting friend clamming last July. When we arrived at the town landing, about four o'clock, I counted forty to fifty people with rakes and buckets in a rather concentrated area about two hundred yards offshore.

We walked out and joined the crowd. Someone told us that since Sunday (the last taking day) some seven bushels of quahogs had been "put" in the vicinity. This would figure out to about thirty-five clams per acre if they had been uniformly distributed in the area—not a very high density—but most had apparently been dumped in concentrated clumps. The aim seemed to be to locate one of these treasure piles and clean it out before anyone else got there. Unfortunately for us, most of the quahogs that had been dumped in sandy areas had already been retrieved, and the remaining ones were largely to be found in the eelgrass beds.

I have not raked in full-grown eelgrass since college days, when I worked at a sailing camp on Pleasant Bay. The grass had to be raked almost daily off the beach and out of the swimming area, a chore that was often given to some of the more unruly campers as punishment. Eelgrass this time of year is over a yard long, thick and slimy, like batches of flat green noodles. Compared with the short nubs of the dormant plants in winter, raking for quahogs in such stuff is unpleasant and extremely difficult—something like combing through the head of some great hairy beast looking for nits.

Most of the quahogs in the grass were still on the surface (not having been there long enough to have dug themselves in) and were most easily located by feeling for them with bare feet. In doing so I suffered numerous nips from buried crabs, and received several minor cuts from broken scallop shells. Once, something flat and rubbery wriggled horribly under my foot and fled—a small flounder or skate, I suspect.

The water in these eelgrass beds was about thigh-high, and growing higher, so that a quahog, once located, had to be retrieved with the rake. This had two disadvantages.

First, it was often difficult to do without entangling the rake tines in the grass and losing the clam. Second, anyone seen energetically wielding his rake, or who was so foolish as to hold up his prize after securing it, was immediately descended upon by nearby clammers who hoped to share in his find.

A more direct though somewhat more grungy method was employed by a few teenage boys. Having located a clump of quahogs, they simply went underwater for them. This technique was as obvious a signal of a find as overt raking, but one that allowed them to secure most of the clams before others could reach them.

There was, however, another, more subtle method which I eventually discovered. I found several good clumps of quahogs in some deep grass, where the water was waist-high. Holding my rake upright and on the bottom, I would place a quahog onto the tines with my foot and then, still holding the clam on the rake with that foot, raise the rake slowly until I could reach the shellfish with my free hand and drop it surreptitiously into my submerged bucket. This was not unlike the method some tennis players use to pick up a ball from the court between racquet and foot without having to bend over.

After a while I got quite adept at this and even devised an improvement. I found I could lift a quahog with one foot onto the top of the other and then flip it directly into the bucket—a sort of slow-motion underwater soccer—without having to move my rake at all.

In such situations one is, in effect, both predator and prey: trying to find and catch the clams without being found out oneself. It was not long before I began to sense that I was not the only one who had stumbled, as it were, upon these methods. Certain other clammers, men and women alike, had a suspiciously unconcerned look on their faces. While most of the people there were stomping or poking assiduously in the grass, or peering about eagle-eyed for a sign of someone else's success, a handful of us seemed merely to be standing around abstractedly in the belly-high water, turning slowly and weaving from side to side with no apparent purpose or direction, as though we had nothing better to do than muck about in these eelgrass jungles and wait for the rising tide to drown us. Only the slow, almost imperceptible raising of someone's clam rake, or the sudden tightening of another's upper torso that betokened some submarine flip of the foot, or a wary meeting and quick separation of glances between two of us, let me know that I had spotted another member in the fraternity of secret quahog collectors.

But it was not until later that night that I realized that I had gained more than a half-bucket of chowder quahogs that afternoon, more than a new pedal motor skill and knowledge of surreptitious human behavior. Using my bare feet as the basic sensory appendage, I had gotten fairly competent at telling the difference between a quahog and a rock, as well as feeling carefully for broken shells before putting my full weight on my foot. My toes had probed like naked, blind worms into the clam's hidden domain, while my head, abstracted, floated in sham idleness above the mildly choppy waters.

Though I received minor cuts and nips in the process, these also represented a new kind of risk in seeking out these mollusks, a risk not experienced when inside the cold-weather shell of heavy rubber waders or hip boots. I had experienced new exposure and contact, and with that contact, knowledge. For it was a tactile knowledge of the flats that I gleaned that afternoon, one I had not known before. As I lay in bed that night, it was my feet, not my eyes or hands, that carried the memory of the day's adventure—the imprint of the ribbed, rounded lumps of the quahogs, the transient scars of sharp, broken clam rims, the pinches and bites of the flats' hidden, furious claws.

An Alewife Lesson

Among schoolchildren last May, I delivered a brief talk on the alewives of the Stony Brook herring run. I have done this for the Cape Cod Museum of Natural History each spring for several years and look forward to it, for it gives me a chance to watch the children react to one of the great seasonal extravagances of the natural world.

I give these talks on the banks of a picturesque, tree-shaded fish ladder at the head of Stony Brook Valley, about a mile inland from Cape Cod Bay. The present fish ladder consists of a series of small concrete locks and pools built in 1948, but for more than three hundred years the inhabitants of our town have used this spot as a source of water power and easily harvested food. Even now the town's old grist mill, originally built in 1660, still stands above the ladder grinding corn for tourists in the summer, and near it in spring local residents gather the alewives in nets for their roe, for pickling, or for garden fertilizer.

The local "herrin'," or alewife (*Alosa pseudoharengus*), is a member of the herring family, which includes shad, menhaden, and the more familiar sea, or sardine, herring. About a foot in length, it is a large-eyed, small-mouthed, silvery-scaled fish with a deep belly. A row of sharp serrations along its ventral ridge has given it the name of "sawbelly" in some areas. Its more common name, alewife, is said to have derived from a loose association of its pronounced abdomen with the ale-wives or female tavernkeepers of Elizabethan England, who were traditionally represented as large-bellied women.

The alewife is an anadromous fish; that is, like the salmon, it makes an annual migration from its saltwater home up coastal rivers and streams to spawn in freshwater ponds and lakes. Beginning with a trickle of individuals and small groups in March, the yearly journey, or run, swells to a flood of millions upon millions of fish by late April or early May as the alewives enter the small brooks and larger estuaries all along the New England coast, pushing upstream to cast their milt and roe (as the sperm and eggs of fish are termed) along the shores of protected ponds and quiet backwaters.

Unlike the larger salmon, most alewives do not die after spawning, at least in the shorter runs. Instead, they return the way they came, back out to the ocean again, where they may travel hundreds of miles during the year before returning to their home stream once again the following spring. The eggs, left to hatch by themselves, develop into herring fry, and about a month after the adults have left, the little alewives, barely two inches long, yield to the current and are also swept seaward. There, a small percentage will survive and in three or four years, using some chemical identification system still poorly understood, will themselves return to spawn in the waters where they were born.

These are some of the facts I try to convey to the children after they have spilled out of the schoolbuses and have been herded into unstable groups by their anxious teachers. Although I give these talks in the name of environmental education, I have few illusions about how much "knowledge" I am conveying in such situations. I am, at most, a convenience, a rack upon which to hang the children's attention briefly. The great thing, of course, is their actually being here, on a day when air, earth, sky, and water are full with the tugging, swaying rawness of spring. Amid the semiformal landscaping of the run, dead fish lie on the banks, their sides gashed open. A brazen black-backed gull vomits in the grass nearby, disgorging indigestible parts of alewife and walking off down the path, black wings crossed behind its back, like a portly old gentleman who cares little for appearances. The children, third- and fourth-graders, focus instinctively on such details, simultaneously fascinated and repelled.

I take them off a way from the stream, to muffle the distractions. I talk a little of the alewife's various names: sawbelly, wall-eye, spring herring, catthrasher, grayback. I speak of its relationship to other members of the herring family. I throw out impressive numbers: 600,000 fish in this small stream each spring, with each female carrying 60,000 to 70,000 eggs. Who can multiply?

I also try to convey some sense of how immediate and important the alewives were to the children here a hundred years ago, when the run was not a tourist attraction but the center of town life, full of mills and factories and food—the pulsing artery of the community.

But this is science and history, distantly real at best. I touch only lightly on the causes and explanations of migration. Explanations, I know, are not important yet. There is no such thing as a mystery to an eight-year-old until an adult presents something as one. The great wonder of these migrating fish, shining in the children's eyes, lies not in our abstract numbers and questions about spawning urges, food chains, or homing instincts, but in the sheer throngs and exuberance of the fish themselves. That is something the children can identify with more closely than with anything I might have to say to them.

Children at this age have an instinctive empathy with the desire for fulfillment. I ask why the fish come up out of the sea to lay their eggs in our freshwater ponds, and a young voice answers, in a somewhat patronizing tone, "Because that's where they're supposed to be born." It occurs to me that an alewife would have given me the same answer.

The children are polite, even attentive, at first. But as I talk I hear the cataract over my shoulder, and the semi-circle of bright young faces begins to disintegrate. A few boys nearest the stream drift off toward it. The teachers and volunteers try valiantly to hold the groups together, but it is like trying to hold the alewives themselves. I can feel myself growing invisible. The children and the fish look right through me and meet somewhere in the water in innocent desire.

It is time, then, to take them to the wooden bridge. I climb down the bank and walk onto the rocks in the stream just above the bridge, stepping across a dark carpet of fish. I net one out of the water and hold it up, high in my rubber-gloved hand, for all to see: a bright, shining, flexing muscle of fish, full of rainbow colors. Only then, with the live fish in my hand, do I put on a bit of magic, drawing all eyes to me.

The children, staring from the bridge, shout down: "Let me feel it!" "If you squeeze it and the bloody stuff comes out, it's a girl!" "Put it back, you're hurting it!" "Catch a boy now!" "Can we catch some?" After a minute I throw the fish back. We watch it float, belly up, for several seconds. "It's dead. You killed it!" Then it turns slowly over, weaves around a bit, disoriented, and joins the flow once more.

Now comes the part I don't like. I must tell the children that they should never handle the fish with bare hands unless they are catching them to take home. That is crucial, I explain, since handling them removes some of the protective oily coating on their scales, exposing them to injury and also to a fungus disease. Even when the children think they are helping the fish by throwing them up the ladder, the alewives may become temporarily traumatized and float far back down the stream before recovering.

These lessons are necessary to stress, I know, but I do not relish my role as a stifler, even in the name of conservation. What I say goes against the children's deepest impulses. What they want, staring down and shouting at me, is not to learn about the fish, but to *join* them. At other, unsupervised times, I have watched them standing in the pools with the alewives, half-accidentally falling in, touching, handling, tossing, and mingling with them —a kind of seasonal baptism and orgy of mindless contact that has occurred each spring here for many generations.

There is, of course, a strong element of cruelty in children and their enthusiasms. I have seen alewives used as baseball bats to hit stones thrown up in the air, or tossed over the mill wheel to crash onto the rocks below, or left alive on the banks, like discarded toys, to thrash and die, gasping and dust-covered. Such things have led many people in town to suggest putting a chain-link fence around the entire area, as has been done at some other runs. Yet despite the abuse and misuse, I cannot help feeling that overall there is something salutary about such close and unfettered contact. The fish come to us already scarred and gashed by the gratuitous savagery of the gulls that swarm farther downstream. Perhaps by netting, grasping, squeezing, bludgeoning them, we too may catch something of the fish's own fire, passed on like some watery torch.

The alternative—sanitary observation—does not strike me as an improvement. Too many times have I seen schoolchildren marched through national parks and wildlife refuges in hushed reverence, so that later, back in the classroom, they may produce beautiful, informed tidbits about nature. This strikes me as the way to teach them that the natural world is only something to be visited, appreciated, and preserved, like an historic relic, rather than wantonly devoured, as it should be at their age. Life demands participation. What we need is not kid gloves, in approved wrappings, but kids' eyes, sharp new eyes to pierce another layer of the mystery. At any rate, we are born wet and are in too far to stay dry.

Finally class is dismissed, and the children go off by themselves, as they have wanted to all along. I am left alone, standing on a rock in the stream, while they splash and laugh and play with the alewives in the pools above and the gulls scream and dive downstream. I think of the centuries-old history of this place, of the comings and goings of man that have left this narrow valley altered but unabated. Most of the old houses and mills are gone. The stone walls, old foundations, and fish ladders remain, providing platforms for our play and curiosity.

Nothing is as it was. Even the trees have grown up again, clothing what was a naked and stone-sprawled landscape a hundred years ago. They testify to the recuperative power of nature to absorb man's works, making even the few new houses that poke their noses pretentiously out over the brow of the valley seem transient, a morning's growth in the play of light and mist, already on the move, sliding down the slopes of time to be carried at last to oblivion.

And yet everything is as it was. The roaring waters plummet unceasingly, the gulls wheel, men and children come to gather the harvest of the season, and Stony Brook, as the poet Conrad Aiken wrote, "ferries its fins to the sea."

For once, I think, the tourist hype is right. Cape Cod *is* one of "America's playgrounds." And so it should be, for the old as well as the young, a place where we can engage in earnest play with the earth, returning its enthusiasms with our own.

The irony is that as the need for this kind of free encounter grows more urgent, the opportunities for it decrease daily. Increasingly we find ourselves forced to restrain ourselves, as I found myself restraining the children in spite of my better instincts. For it is not our impulses that are bad, but the manner and scale on which we have chosen to express them. By our machines and our sheer numbers, by our appetite and ability to be everywhere and see everything, we strain the capacities of such places as this. We watch our play grow deadly in its effects until we are forced to put up more and more fences, more and more limits, and so at last lose the birthright of contact we so sorely need.

What the Stones Said

(for the Chatham Chorale)

I would know my shadow and my light,
So shall I at last be whole.

—Sir Michael Tippett,
A Child of Our Time

O N T H U R S D A Y N I G H T , following choir practice, I drove back by way of Nickerson State Park.
I was in no rush to get home. "Hill Street Blues" was a
repeat, and I was still full of the music and words of
Tippett's oratorio, awed by his power to forge such deep
beauty out of the world's terror and suffering during
those first dark years of World War II in England.

So I turned off into the park and drove down the unlit
winding road to the small boat landing on the shores of
Cliff Pond. Despite recent rains, the water level in the
pond was still down, leaving a wide band of exposed
beach around its perimeter. It was a clear, calm night,

a few degrees below freezing, the full moon quarter-risen above the surrounding rim of dark, undulating hills. From the southeast, distant but clearly audible, came the sounds of rock music being played loudly on a radio —a car radio, I guessed, parked in one of the campgrounds somewhere beyond the pond. It varied in volume and carried cleanly through the night, though somehow I did not find it obtrusive. It sounded as if the dark hills themselves were singing.

The world turns on its dark side.
It is winter.

Though it had dropped below freezing for the past several nights, the broad waters of Cliff Pond remained unfrozen and almost perfectly still. They mirrored, in moonlight, the low, dark hills on the far western shore like a statement of perfect peace and contentment, the fulfilled stillness of a long, hushed, fermataed closing chord.

I walked the perimeter of the pond, something over two and a half miles, in about an hour, and during the entire circuit I neither saw nor heard a single wintering duck on its surface, not out in its center, not in the long southern coves, not even in any of the little cut-off side ponds. It was as though the pond had dismissed them, and all animated life, in order to make this pure statement of itself, unblurred by any moving details.

This is the hardest of all sounds in nature to hear: the silent assertion of a landscape itself. It requires a rare confluence of moods—clarity on nature's part, receptiveness on our own—a suspension of normal expectations and a relaxed extension of our senses, to feel such deep vibrations.

I walked south, clockwise around the pond, along an exposed shore several yards wide. The recent rains seemed to have sunk in, and the water level to have receded again, leaving a hardened, slick path of frozen ground around its rim. In the shallow water along the shore only the reflection of a single star, jiggling slowly up and down as though on an elastic string, betrayed any agitation in the pond.

Looking up, I found the star's original counterpart in the sky above the southern coves: the blinking, ice-blue chip of Sirius. To its right the faint outline of Orion rose late above the hills, as though weary and drained by his nightly climbs through the winter skies. Even Sirius was somewhat paled by the moonlight, though quite near it an even brighter star—Jupiter or Venus—shone in companionable splendor. It was the day after planetary syzygy, the day after the end of the world. Along the crest of the hills the bone-white disk of the moon sliced through the stiff pines.

Man has measured the heavens with a telescope,
driven the gods from their thrones.
But the soul, the soul watching the chaotic mirror,
knows that the Gods return.

The moonlight, rather than illuminating, seemed to cloak the visible world, reducing everything to vague, generalized outlines. By contrast, the world of sound seemed to sharpen and clarify as I walked. I became more conscious of my feet, especially along the rocky or cobbled shores that characterize the northeastern corners of the coves, their stones driven or plowed up onto the beaches by northwest wind and ice. Beneath my steps, the stones seemed like voices, human voices, struck into sound by my passage. The larger, bread-loaf-sized stones uttered mute complaints and silent groans, as though the compact and compressed history of their existence, normally quelled by day and smothered with water, were released by the dead moonlight.

We all believe as children, and sometimes later, that the earth is quick with unperceived life, released at night. As the sun's warmth quickens that which moves and grows by day, so to human imagination the moon's cold light gives life to inanimate forms, to rocks, stones, and sticks. Now its perfect, passive illumination seemed to release the voice, the implicit eloquence of shape and endless transformation inherent in all unmoving, moved things.

Deep in the long coves there were stretches of smaller stones along the beach, ones only slightly larger than pebbles, that virtually startled me with their panicky excitement as I passed. Farther up on the beach a group of larger rocks, small boulders really, their tops partially hoary with lichen, held aloof counsel together. They made me feel like an eavesdropper, and I could almost hear them pause in their conversation as I passed.

> *The dark forces rise like a flood.*
> *Men's hearts are heavy: they cry for peace.*

Strewn here and there along the exposed shore were sections of dead pine trunks I had never noticed before, barkless and supine beneath the moon. Drowned and felled in a time of high water past, they too seemed to cry out in agony, like tortured shapes. One long section, spiked with short broken-off branches, looked like some giant upturned caterpillar. Yet at the same time the sinuous musculature of its silvered grain stood out expressively in the moonlight and gave it the aspect of a human torso, truncate of limbs and arching up from the cold stones, so that I found myself turning away from its naked suffering.

I was amazed at how many times I must have passed these shapes, unremarked, by day. Now I could not bear to look closely at them, so piteously did they cry out.

Along the northeastern point of the westernmost cove someone had lifted some of the rocks and piled them in a line to form a short miniature jetty that protruded a few feet down into the water. It ran out like a short play, but one that used real people for actors, and it was silent. To the north, on the ridge across the pond, the state forestry camp glowed soundlessly like some distant hill city. At the head of the cove I rang the branches of a shrubby swamp maple growing along the shore; they clacked icily, but said nothing.

Then a curious thing happened. As I looked up again at Sirius, I noticed a bright reddish star below it that had not been there earlier. Mars, I thought; but it was much brighter than Mars. After a minute or two I realized that the star was moving perceptibly, though not visibly —like the minute hand of a clock—in relation to Sirius, gradually rising and at last gaining ascendancy over it. A satellite, I thought, probably Communist.

I remembered, twenty years ago, how we went outside to watch the first *Sputnik*s and *Telstar*s, how fascinated we were to see these new stars moving so swiftly against the grain of the slow-wheeling night. We even danced to songs about them. Now I resented the smooth apparent motion of the satellite as a harbinger of a future sky cross-hatched and gridded over with man-made lights and weapons. It rose several degrees a minute, and was as bright as any star in the sky; yet when I looked again a few minutes later, it was gone.

> *The cold deepens.*
> *The world descends into the icy waters,*
> *Where lies the jewel of great price.*

Along the northwest shore of the pond, perhaps because it is more protected from the wind, the water at the edge was beginning to freeze. In a ragged band anywhere from a few inches to several feet wide, the ice was extending its teeth out from the edge in Jack Frost window patterns. It was still just the barest film of ice, so thin that when I detached one of the newly formed shards and lifted it toward my mouth, it melted and fell from between my fingers, shattering into a billion bits on the hardened beach.

Earlier, along the open shores, I had played with the moon in the water, making its reflected disk skip along the smooth shore edge like a flat stone. Now I dragged its image through the burgeoning arsenal of ice growing in the water, ripping it through phalanxes of knives, fishbone spines, and jack-o'-lantern teeth.

> *The words of wisdom are these:*
> *Winter cold means inner warmth,*
> *the secret nursery of the seed.*

At last I was nearing the Big Rocks, a pair of enormous glacial erratics situated near the northwest corner of the pond. Normally the lower of the two boulders sits several feet in the water, but now both lay completely beached. I approached them with a growing anticipation mixed with apprehension. I could not conceive what profound cries or utterances such towering forms might make, and was ready to cover my ears, if necessary.

But unexpectedly, they did not speak at all. Rather, they *sang*—softly, with all the reserve of their great masses and strength: a high, falsetto song, arched and drawn out, such as great whales make, unheard by us, beneath their sea. It seemed not only to contain all previous sounds made by the rocks and fallen trees, but to carry the cry of all creation, deteriorating like a cherished face in the rain of time.

Their enormous, ice-rounded bulks moved through the night like the measures of their song. I followed them as far as I dared, and it seemed that if a wind had come up then, I might have been swept away for good.

I think it is only at times of such extraordinary outer calm, and inner fullness, that we hear such voices in nature. Remembered by day, they embarrass us, like disturbing dreams. We tell no one and make conscious efforts to forget them, nailing up lights on wooden crosses along such dark stretches of our thoroughfares, to prevent them from recurring.

We move through our days on a kind of automatic pilot, unaware of how tightly we hold ourselves in and apart from one another, how much stress and resistance are involved in keeping a steady course against the universal winds. But here, for an hour, all winds seemed to cease, the multifarious sounds they muffle were released, and nature's unstrung voices made themselves heard in the dark silence.

The moving waters renew the earth.
It is spring.

As I approached the landing, the spears of ice along the pond's edge gradually drew in and disappeared, and water once more met the shore. Now the slightest wind came up. Its moon-edged ripples were just barely visible out from shore, yet it was enough to cloud the pond surface, to silence the beach, and to keep the hills from answering themselves. From somewhere far off, in an unseen tree, a single crow cawed high and sharp, breaking the night.

A Beach for All Seasons

T HE FIRST AND only time I saw Henry Beston
was on a bright, crisp fall day in 1964, outside the
recently completed Eastham Visitors Center of the Cape
Cod National Seashore. Surrounding him were the U.S.
Secretary of the Interior, the Governor of Massachusetts,
the Vice-President of the Massachusetts Audubon Society,
various local dignitaries, and we, the curious and admir-
ing public. We were all gathered there for ceremonies
honoring the author of *The Outermost House* and dedi-
cating his famous beach cottage at the lower end of
Coast Guard Beach as a National Literary Landmark.

Beston, at seventy-two, was already an invalid and a
dying man. He sat in the bright October sun in a wheel-
chair, covered with a lap robe and wrapped in a scarf,
wearing his characteristic tweed jacket and beret and
sporting a neat, clipped gray moustache. He sat quietly,
without speaking, but his eyes were clear and alert and
still expressed that Gallic charm he cultivated so
effectively.

Others spoke, though much of what they said was

whipped away on a sharp northerly wind. Later a beach buggy caravan carrying Beston and the politicians drove down the inside sand road of Coast Guard Beach to the "Fo'castle"—as he called his little house—where a brass plaque was affixed to its front wall. Some of us followed, making a slower pilgrimage down the beach on foot. I remember being perplexed when I read the curious inscription on the plaque that someone had chosen to commemorate Beston's stay there thirty-seven years before:

"THE OUTERMOST HOUSE" IN WHICH HENRY BESTON, AUTHOR-NATURALIST, WROTE HIS CLASSIC BOOK BY THAT NAME WHEREIN HE SOUGHT THE GREAT TRUTH AND FOUND IT IN THE NATURE OF MAN.

Surely, I thought, Beston must have been embarrassed to be suspected of seeking anything as pretentious as "the Great Truth," whatever that is. And if he found any, it lay not in "the Nature of Man," but in the man of nature he became on this isolated barrier spit as he experienced and chronicled "the noble ritual of the burning year."

Henry Beston died four years later at his beloved farm in Nobleboro, Maine, but over the years, on the many subsequent walks I made down the length of Coast Guard Beach, the Outermost House remained something of a goal, a benchmark for gradual change and a symbol of gentle continuity.

At first I knew nothing of the mechanics of barrier beach movement, though the processes of change were clear enough even to an untutored eye. It was satisfaction enough, in early spring, to take the first walk of the season down the outside of the beach as the new spears of beach grass were beginning to poke through last year's dry, wind-shredded stalks. Some years the fore-slopes of the dunes looked smooth and untouched, their sculptured flanks dusted with graceful corduroy patterns of purple magnetite thrown up by the tides. At other times, especially after late winter storms, the dunes presented a sheer sand wall, clawed twelve feet high in places, yet still knitted together by the exposed roots of beach grass, tough, knotty fibers up to eight feet long, which even in death continued to hold these sandy bulwarks together like a grid of reinforcement rods.

At a certain break in the line of dunes, a little over a mile south of the Seashore's public parking lot, I would cross over to the back side of the beach where the Fo'castle, as unpretentious as ever, sat nestled in a protected little hollow beside the marsh. It never was the "Outermost House," in the sense of being the last structure on the beach. Even in Beston's day there were several gunning cabins farther down the spit, and during the late sixties and early seventies as many as ten summer dwellings, most of much more recent date, sat on either side of his cottage. The title of his book referred not to linear geography but to ultimate exposure.

Nor was the Outermost House in its original position. It had been moved back from the sea twice since it was built and had been given a new chimney and foundation. Once I found what likely had been the house's original well pipe sticking up out of the sand on the lower beach, but it was gone the following spring. Beston's cottage may well have been the only traveling National Literary Landmark in existence.

Still, despite these obvious changes, there were some reassuring continuities. Often I found starlings perched on the house's chimney. During the late 1920s Beston had observed these birds, then relative newcomers to the Eastham moors, and wondered, "Will the various flocks now inhabiting the moors mingle to form one enormous and tyrannous confederacy?" Time seems to have proved his fears unfounded, for though starlings have increased everywhere, their numbers on the Cape appear to have stabilized at relatively low levels, in large part because of the disappearance of fields and meadows and the regrowth of forests.

Frequently I saw a large brown form with a white tail swooping low out over the grass islands of the marsh: a female harrier. In *The Outermost House* Beston describes a female marsh hawk, as it was called then, which regularly visited these dunes and marshes when he lived here, and I would imagine that this bird was the direct descendant of the one he saw, that some natural ties continued to weave, unbroken, down through the years.

In winter and spring I could go up to the house and inspect its current status, noting its casual framing, its flimsy foundation, and the brick chimney that seemed to grow up through the floor out of the sand. I could not help thinking that such a structure wouldn't stand a chance of passing today's building code requirements. Yet would stronger floor joists and taller ceilings ever give us a firmer foundation in nature than was achieved in this shack by its first occupant?

During the summer and fall months the structure was usually occupied, for it had become the property of Massachusetts Audubon and was rented out to members and their families. It always pleased me to see it being used thus, to see clothes drying on the line and hear chatter coming from its small porch. It never was suited for guided, reverent tours, and continued use seemed the best of commemorations that could be bestowed upon it. I often thought of staying there myself sometime, but whether because the waiting lists were too long or because it was simply too easy to walk out there anytime, I never did.

When I eventually began writing about the place where I lived, I learned something about the nature and history of this beach. Though all barrier beaches perform a similar function of sheltering estuaries and marshes that lie behind them, each is unique in its character and dynamics. Coast Guard Beach is part of a two-pronged barrier spit system. It stretches southward from the old Eastham Coast Guard Station (now a National Seashore Environmental Education Center) in a low line of undulating dunes averaging fifteen to twenty-five feet in height. To the south its partner, Nauset Spit, stretches northward from Nauset Beach in Orleans. The distance between the mainland ends of these two spits is almost three miles, but their tips nearly meet at Nauset Inlet, a narrow opening through which the tide pours and pulls in swift, tumbling currents into Nauset Marsh, Nauset Harbor, and eventually to the head of Town Cove at Orleans Center, three and a half miles inland.

One of the things that makes Nauset Inlet such a dangerous crossing for the lobster and fishing boats that use it is that it is a migrating inlet, one that over the years has moved considerable distances north and south in a rough cyclical pattern. At this point on the Cape's Atlantic coastline, the offshore or longshore current is from north to south. Shaped and fed by these sand-filled currents, Coast Guard Beach normally lengthens over a period of years, while Nauset Spit correspondingly shrinks, until at some point the ocean breaks through to the north, the lower part of Coast Guard Beach attaches itself to Nauset Spit, and the whole process begins again. Thus Coast Guard Beach acts like a growing finger, repeatedly amputated yet constantly regenerating, time and time again.

In addition to these cyclical fluctuations, Coast Guard Beach, like most Atlantic barrier systems, is a retreating beach. Over the centuries it has kept pace with the receding glacial bluffs to the north, using the material eroded from those bluffs and carried southward by ocean currents to build new lines of dunes on its landward side as its own seaward wall wears away. The present dune line is thought to be over a quarter-mile farther inland than it was when Samuel de Champlain first sailed into Nauset Harbor in 1605.

Despite the continual changes wrought on this beach as long as people have known it, few of us anticipated the extent of destruction and alteration caused by the great storm of February 7–8, 1978.

Its effects on this beach were spectacular and unprecedented: nearly 80 percent of the protective dune ridge was flattened or heavily gouged; enormous overwashes of sand were spread out into Nauset Marsh; the National Seashore's large parking lot and bathhouse were obliterated; and most of the remaining beach cottages were destroyed, several of them being carried out into the marsh or even clear across to the western shore, over a mile away.

That February storm serves as a major benchmark, not only in the history of Coast Guard Beach, but in the personal lives of those of us who witnessed it. As at the outbreak of a war or the shooting of a president, most of us can remember where we were and what we were doing during those two days, when record tides and near-hurricane winds combined to invade and overwhelm the land in almost unprecedented dimensions.

I did not reach Coast Guard Beach until the second day of the storm, when a strange calm, an almost spring-like mist and warmth, filled the air above the beach. I stood with the large crowd that had gathered below the old station and was cheering each tremendous, milky swell as it rolled in and battered the bathhouse, surged over the drowned parking lot, and then continued on out into the flooded marsh. Farther south, beyond the wide cut-through forced by the ocean, the beach was littered with the debris and wreckage of cottages and their contents, along with the stranded and broken shells of ten thousand sea clams.

Earlier that day a friend of mine had called and asked, "Did you hear that the Outermost House perished?" His choice of words was highly appropriate, I thought, for its passing seemed to deserve a term usually reserved for souls, thoughts, and principles of human liberty. Its remains had been swept out to sea through Nauset Inlet the previous night, though the brass plaque and, ironically, the outhouse were later recovered.

Now, standing with the crowd and looking out over the once-again-altered beach, I thought that Beston would have assented, even approved of the Fo'castle's fate. He had no expectations for its immortality. He knew where it was he lived. The house had been but the shell for the book, which he established on imperishable foundations.

It has been several years now since that memorable storm, and things continue to change at Coast Guard

Beach. Only two of the beach cottages near the north end remain, and these have been heavily damaged by subsequent storms. A third was rebuilt much farther south on four-foot piers, sitting like some squat spider out on the flat overwash plain. Though unprotected by dunes, it may actually last the longest, since it allows the high tides to wash under rather than over it.

There has been a ban on vehicular traffic on the beach since the storm, and even pedestrian access has been limited to the outside beach to allow the dunes to recover. Though plans for rebuilding the public parking lot in a safer location were drawn up by the National Seashore as early as the summer following the storm, no construction has yet taken place. Except for a stormwatcher's overlook behind the Coast Guard Station which is open in winter, the nearest parking area is a small lot at Doane Rock Picnic Area, over a half-mile away. Otherwise, to reach the beach one must hike or bike along the trails from the Visitors Center, two miles away, or ride one of the shuttle buses operated from there in the summer. Though these buses are free and run every fifteen minutes, and though lifeguards and portable restrooms are provided at the beach, the buses are sparsely used. Most tourists seem to prefer to drive and pay for the convenience of parking at much more crowded beaches elsewhere.

Despite these restrictions on human actions, the beach does not appear to have recovered much from the damage of the 1978 storm. Only a few remnants of the original dune line remain, and overwashes by the ocean at the former parking lot site are still regular occurrences in winter. It is possible that the dune line will never reestablish itself to its previous extent and that the cyclical extensions of the northern spit have been permanently altered. If so, the long-term consequences for Nauset Marsh and for the mainland to the west may be significant.

Yet, visiting the beach one day last winter, I had to admit that much of the harsh, ragged look of the remaining dune walls had softened considerably since the storm. Many of the breaks in the dune lines had filled in with several feet of wind-blown sand, and vegetation had begun to move down the sides of the cuts, so that these features once again began to take on the sculpted lines of dunes rather than the look of broken ramparts.

Things age quickly here, but they also heal quickly, rounding off, filling in, growing over, taking on the contours of the human form again. Unlike barren rocky mountain peaks that stand in opposition to the forces that break them down, growing rougher each year, cracking and splintering anew with each frost and thaw, the strategy of the dunes is accommodation, prostration, if necessary, allowing the enemy to penetrate and destroy and then building anew on the foundations he has laid down.

On the inner side of the spit, the storm surges had mixed large amounts of plant debris with sand, scattering several small driftline mounds out into the marsh. Growing out of these miniature islands were incipient communities of new beach plants—sea rocket, beach grass, dusty miller, and others—the beginnings of a new line of dunes. Looking at this life emergent from unprecedented destruction, I wondered if Beston, were he here now, would have recognized this quintessential expression of his own concluding observation, that "Creation is here and now."

· · ·

Meanwhile, for those willing to give up the privilege of buying gas and paying parking fees, Coast Guard Beach remains accessible in summer by foot, bicycle, or bus. One day last July I took the shuttle bus from the Visitors Center, the same place from which I first left to walk the beach two decades before. There were perhaps a dozen other riders, most of them older, retired persons. The bus took about five minutes to reach the beach, depositing us at the foot of the station hill.

It was a beautiful summer's day, hot but with a light, cooling sea breeze. Perhaps a hundred people were spread out along the entire length of the beach. The sun glinted off the low, curling surf as off a knife blade. Summer was, to use Beston's phrase, at "high tide." The sides of the dunes were covered with the full-blown, dark-green bouquets of beach grass, soft pale clusters of dusty miller, and the spreading vines of beach pea dotted with dark purple blossoms. Savannah sparrows darted among the beach plum and the beach grass. A new least tern colony had established itself on the site of the former parking lot, and on some of the snow fencing surrounding the colony a few horned larks mixed their high, tinkling songs with the sharper *keck-keck* warning calls of the nesting terns. Nearby, in the lush green marsh to the west, a trio of fat, sleek Canada geese grazed over the meadow grass, waddling along with the slow, rhythmic gait of cattle.

The older couples, carrying blankets and other beach gear, began to make their way out over the sands. Shy and timid, almost like young lovers, they held hands as they helped one another down to the beach. I followed along behind. After so many years, so many storms, so many unceasing changes, this still seems like a good place to begin.

Cutting In

SIXTY-FIVE PILOT WHALES, ranging in size from five to eighteen feet, beached themselves Tuesday night in the salt marsh on the south side of Lieutenant's Island in Wellfleet Harbor. It was said to be the largest stranding of whales on Cape Cod in over a quarter-century. By Thursday morning a police cruiser was stationed at the entrance to the wooden bridge leading onto the island. The roadblock was not to protect the whales, which by then were all quite dead, but rather to keep the fragile salt marsh from being trampled by the hundreds of curious onlookers who were beginning to arrive from as far away as New York and Vermont.

From the bridge one could see the black, bulky forms of the whales looming out in the marsh several hundred yards away and, bending over them, staff members of the New England Aquarium and the Wellfleet Bay Audubon Sanctuary (which owns the marsh), who since dawn had been dissecting and autopsying the corpses. A yellow helicopter from Channel 4 Newspeak landed near them and, like some giant wasp laying eggs on the beach, deposited a camera crew and took off again. At the entrance to the marsh area an exhausted aquarium staff member in bloodstained pants sat against a cedar post fence. Next to him, tacked to a pole, was a copy of the Federal Marine Mammal Act regulations stating that stranded whales were federal property and that anyone caught tampering with them was subject to a $10,000 fine.

Nearly all of the sixty-five whales had stranded close together in a stretch of marsh about 150 yards long. They started coming ashore late Tuesday afternoon during the extreme high tide of the new moon and became trapped high up in the marsh when the tide receded. Efforts were made to push them off, but without success. All through the night the whales could be heard breathing in concert with a strangled, moaning noise. By Wednesday morning all but ten of the whales were dead, their lungs crushed by the weight of their bodies. The rest were given injections of sodium pentabarbital when it became clear there was no possibility of saving them. The only survivor was a young 750-pound female which had been taken to the Marine Life Aquarium in Mystic, Connecticut. She was listed in critical but stable condition.

(A week later a call was received from a woman in Hyannis who said she was a psychic. She said she had been having strange dreams and that she had realized the dreams were coming from the whale in Mystic. She said that she had learned that the whales had stranded because they lock on telepathically to the herd leader, that the leader had become sick and beached itself, and that the others had followed. The way to prevent these strandings, she said, was to identify the leader when it comes ashore and kill it, breaking the mental hold on the herd. She said the dreams were filled with intense loneliness.)

On Thursday morning the tide was coming in again, though it would not reach the whales this time. The carcasses had been numbered, from west to east, by carving Roman numerals four inches high into their sides just behind the ear holes (Roman because straight lines are easier to cut with a knife than curved Arabic numerals). These scratches constantly emitted thin red lines of decomposing gas bubbles. (During the last century, when blackfish strandings were more common and more desirable, local residents claimed possession of the beached animals by carving their initials in similar fashion, though often while the whales were still alive.) Whale Number III, a large male nearly eighteen feet long, lay on his side with his penis bloated and extended into the shape of a fantastic curved horn over two feet long, sheathed in a shiny, flaking, thin membrane, as though it were painted with silver metallic paint. Most of the whales' penises, however, were invisible, retracted into the vulvalike genital openings, so that the males could only be told from the females by the lack of teats on either side of the opening. Some of the tongues had protruded in death and had been partially pecked away by gulls and crows.

Each whale was all black, except for two large smudged patches of white, one directly below the lower jaw, the other around the genital opening. At first one does not see the eye, for it is black too, and the head, blunt and round, looks like a blind battering ram with a curved, skewed line of a mouth running back on each side like a smirking scar. But the eye is there, walnut-sized and blue-black, just behind and above the back of the mouthline. Most of the eyes had clear, mucuslike secretions running out of them that might have been mistaken for tears. The faces had that simplified, harmless, neotenic, abstract look that we tend to ascribe to benevolent celluloid aliens, which perhaps explains some of our recent affectionate attitudes toward cetaceans. They look like enormous embryos.

They lay side by side in groups of three to five whales of various sizes, like families, or else singly, some drooped halfway into potholes in the marsh, others wedged into small tidal creeks, forming natural bridges for the autopsy crews to get from one section of the marsh to another. There were ten people working on the whales, plus another dozen media people carrying video cameras, large cloth-covered mikes, and clipboards.

The smell was not too bad yet. Eight of the whales had been cut open. Some had been stripped of their blubber with long, wood-handled flensing knives, revealing long, striated, marble flanks of deep red muscle, like prime steak. Others had been decapitated with crosscut saws, their large heads lying around like huge black watermelons with bright-red cut ends. Still others had been sliced ventrally open, releasing cascades of greenish-white, sausagelike intestines, large green pouchlike stomachs, and other viscera down onto the marsh. Several of the marsh pools between the whales were deep red with blood and filled with floating chunks of discarded whale meat and organs, like grisly seafood chowders.

Other carcasses had the tips of their tails or flippers lopped off, or a square patch of flesh several inches square cut neatly out of their sides, like a small hatch or window. Most lay on their sides, parallel to the shore, at the upper edge of the marsh. More than anything else they looked like airplane fuselages that had lost their wings, aerodynamic and immovable, hard and rubbery, resistant to the touch.

The Audubon director and two other men stomped back across the marsh carrying bagged samples of stained blubber from one whale that had stranded apart from the main mass in a small tidal creek a quarter-mile away. Another worker was digging into a stomach pouch of tomalleylike material containing shrimp shells and squid beaks. He was dictating to a woman standing beside him holding a clipboard: "A small ulcer here, maybe two centimeters across, partially calcified . . ."

On others, sections of jaw containing four or five teeth had been sawed out with hacksaws. The teeth are quite small, less than an inch long in all but the largest individuals.

One man in his early thirties had been dissecting marine mammals for nine years and had performed over one thousand autopsies. He seemed very practiced at it, making latitudinal cuts sixteen inches apart along a whale's side, then expertly flensing the two-inch-thick strip of blubber while another man pulled it back with a meathook, in a manner similar to the way one chisels out a mortise for a door hinge. As he cut through the torso of one large male, however, he pierced the inner skin, and the built-up gas exploded, sending up a large red spout of blood with a loud *whoosh*—exactly like the sound of a whale exhaling. Someone shouted, "Thar she blows!," several others yelled "Upwind! Upwind!," and everyone scurried out of harm's way.

Meanwhile, the interviews and filming went on in various spots on the marsh. In addition to several of the Boston television stations, all three major networks had dispatched crews to the site. A CBS crew was attempting to tape commentary by a newscaster standing in front of some of the whales ("Scientists remain in the dark as to the reasons for such . . ."), but a sightseeing plane from Provincetown repeatedly buzzed in close behind him, and after five or six takes they gave up. A Channel 7 newsman was interviewing the Audubon director, who was saying that he had been the first to discover the whales on Tuesday evening just after returning from a meeting; he was in sneakers and dress pants but had just slogged into the marsh and that was it. They had trouble with this one, too; an orange Channel 5 copter with large blue numbers kept circling into view (no free advertising of rival stations). Despite these problems, most of the people, scientists and journalists alike, seemed quiet, respectful, businesslike, and diligent. Only one woman, one of the few year-round residents on the island, called it a tragedy.

By late morning the rising tide slowly drove everyone off the beach and across the marsh. Back at the fenced entrance the posted regulations had blown down and lay in the mud. A woman from the New England Aquarium said that they would be at it at least another day and would probably try to "drag it out as long as we can." Eventually, though, the remains would have to be left in the marsh. Unlike most whale beachings, where the bodies are either towed out to sea or buried on the beach with bulldozers, boats could not get close enough to haul these carcasses off and there was no way to get large machinery out there without severely damaging the marsh. The plan was to cut up the remaining bodies and place them in the numerous marsh potholes, in the hope that they would work themselves down into the peat over the winter.

Some of the nearby residents were dubious of this strategy, afraid of an overpowering stench the following summer. Some of the local shellfishermen expressed concern that the rotting carcasses would harm clam and oyster stocks, whose larvae develop in these marshes. But one of the scientists dismissed this, saying, "Marshes are naturally very nutrient-rich, you know." On the beach the gulls and the crows marked time, waiting for us to leave.

North Beach Journal

I

I HAVE BEEN LIVING alone for three days now in a cottage on the west shore of North Beach, a long and narrow barrier spit of low sand dunes and salt marsh lying a mile or so east of Chatham at the elbow of Cape Cod. Chatham is one of the fog capitals of New England, especially in spring. Since I arrived on Sunday evening the fog has poured nearly continuously over this naked beach like some great silent river; but late this afternoon the wind shifted to the west and the gray shroud at last began to lift.

I do not live alone easily. In solitude I find myself inordinately affected by the weather. It is as though meteorology takes the place of intimate company, and the distinction between outer weather and inner mood is gradually obliterated. In such situations it is not so much a question of trying to give myself over to nature as trying to hold something back, some bit of perspective and self-evaluation. This is just what fog loves to steal from you.

There was already a dense fog at the water's edge and a light northwest wind blowing when I set off about 5:00 P.M. last Sunday in a small red rowboat from Scatteree Town Landing on the Chatham mainland. My wife Beth and daughter Katy were there assisting and forming a farewell committee. Within a few minutes their forms dissolved and melted into the ghostly background of low bluffs and houses, and soon that, too, disappeared.

According to the map I had, the cottage lay across Pleasant Bay about a mile to the southeast, at the northern end of a group of twenty or so beach cottages known as the South Colony. I steered by compass, due east, to compensate for the southerly push of wind. A small squadron of terns flew close by heading north, gray on gray over gray.

Rowing is a strange method of traveling, even within the contained waters of a pond. One is always pulling oneself backward, into the unknown, steering by what one has already experienced or left behind. Here, in an open-ended estuary, with no visible landmarks, I had the curious feeling that I was rowing into the center of my own mind where figures vanished and loomed like memory.

I passed a pair of channel markers and heard the deep thrum of a motor approaching from the south. It turned out to be Buzz Hutchins, a bulldozer operator who had dug my house foundation a few years ago.

"Hello, Robert, where you going?" he called out cordially. Cape Codders are rarely surprised by anything they find at sea.

"Cabin," I yelled back, jerking my head toward the

outer beach as I kept rowing, and he disappeared with a wave back into my past.

Fifteen minutes later I stopped to check my compass bearings. Though the bay at this point is relatively shallow and not very wide, it is notoriously deceptive in fog with backcurrents and sudden shifts in wind. The water around me appeared calm, quiet, and completely empty. I had wanted to cut ties for the duration, but not this quickly.

Suddenly the water was filled with the pulsing bodies of moon jellies, domed and translucent, drifting north with the incoming tide over beds of dark, streaming eelgrass. I reached out and stroked a long, slick frond of grass. A biological oddity, eelgrass is a true marine flowering plant descended from some terrestrial angiosperm which, like the land ancestors of whales and walruses, has returned for some reason to the sea. What are you doing out here, grass, among jellyfish and seabirds? Where are we all heading?

After a half-hour or so of rowing and neck-twisting, I finally saw a beach materializing behind me, still vague and undefined in the fog. The large, dark silhouette of a cottage loomed straight ahead. I could not believe my blind luck in hitting it on the mark. But when I came ashore, the building did not fit the description at all.

I wandered around the ghostly dunes for some time before stumbling upon a family at another cottage, packing up their Blazer and about to leave after a weekend's vacation. They told me I had landed, not at the South Colony, but at the North Colony, a second cottage group nearly a half-mile north of where I wanted to be.

I had erred twice, it seems: first, in not taking into account the push of the incoming tide, and second, in not correcting my compass readings for magnetic declination—some sixteen degrees at this longitude—a stupid, amateur's mistake.

By the time I returned to the boat, the light had begun to fail and it was raining lightly. I set off again, rowing south against the tide just a few yards offshore. The fog now alternately closed in and lifted, revealing at brief intervals the dim outline of the mainland across the bay, ridiculously close. Black-bellied plovers and small sand-pipers lined the water's edge, probing the tideline with short, dark bills. Fog and dusk were thickening to dark-ness when I finally came to the cottage, pulled into a little cove just south of it, and hauled the boat ashore.

The beach cottage belongs to a neighbor of mine, Tia Tonis, who had offered me the use of it for a week. She had taken my heavier gear down by jeep on Saturday and had returned to the mainland that afternoon. When I entered the cottage I found my trunk full of food and books set against one wall, and on the table a nice wel-coming note from Tia with a pair of sharpened pencils.

It was too late to begin lighting the gas lamps or cook-ing a meal, so I made myself a sandwich by candlelight, and threw a sleeping bag on one of the cots and myself after it. All around me was the dull roar of wind and surf, and an occasional compacted thud of a breaker on the ocean side of the beach a quarter-mile away. The tide was still rising. The fog had lifted again, and now, to the southwest, across the dark waters of Pleasant Bay, the great double beams of Chatham Light raced out into the night, chasing one another like demons up the dark strip of the outer beach until they broke against the south wall of the house, exploding in star-shaped flashes through the screens.

This place is now home, I thought, my neighborhood for a week. It has the feeling of being wholly contained in nature, of existing within her terms. What a strange crossing it has been! Never could I have gotten so swiftly detached from the mainland, emotionally and psychologically, under clear skies. Lying here now at night on this open strand, listening to the dull roar of the surf and the unobstructed wind, it seems years since this morning when I was down in the bog below our house, only a few miles from here, gathering the eggs of wood frogs and salamanders beneath a thick forest canopy, finding woodland lady slippers and trailing arbutus, listening to the calls of ovenbirds and other woodland warblers, and the strange whistles of wood ducks in the bog.

There are other cottages nearby this one, but they are all dark. There are no other lights as far as I can see up or down the length of the beach. Now the fog has closed in again, this time for good, it seems, and not even the drumming demon-beam of Chatham Light can pierce it.

II

I like this house, its bright, spare, unfinished look. It is a shell: twenty-four by twenty-eight feet, shingled and roofed on the outside, with studded walls pierced everywhere by the exposed tips of shingle nails, a trussed and strapped ceiling, open doorless partitions where the bedrooms will be, and a bare plywood floor.

The house sits about sixty yards from the gentle waters of the bay. Like many beach cottages, this one seems largely an excuse for windows. There are five on the west side, facing the bay, two on the south, three on the east, two on the north, plus three windowed steel doors. One large white table sits in the center of the unpartitioned area—for the typewriter and "heavy work"—

with a smaller pine table next to the west windows, complete with two ice-cream parlor twisted-wire chairs, for meals, reading, journalizing, and bay-watching. A few white curtains hang on rods above the windows, more to wave inward in the breeze than to veil anything. There is a gas stove, three gas lights, a gas refrigerator, a hand pump and sink, and a flush toilet in the outhouse. The refrigerator has been acting up a little. It won't shut off, so I disconnect it now and then. I wish I had brought an onion.

In exchange for the use of the house I have agreed to paint the wood trim, window sashes, and screens. Four gallons of white paint were left stacked in one of the partitioned rooms. I planned to begin Monday morning, but when I woke at dawn the fog and mist still clung tenaciously around the house. After breakfast I decided to take a walk across to the ocean shore, hoping it would burn off by afternoon.

North Beach is about a thousand feet wide here, a terrain of low dunes and wet swales, with a higher broken ridge of primary dune just before the outer beach. At no point does the land rise twenty feet above sea level.

This barrier beach has undergone more changes than most: lengthening, contracting, breaking up into archipelagoes of sandy islets, dissolving and re-forming again every couple of hundred years. Though the spit is at present some ten miles long and extends over four miles south of the Tonis cottage, the section of dune I was now walking was a harbor entrance into Pleasant Bay a hundred years ago. Until last fall a large, turreted wooden building stood just behind the first ridge of dunes—the Old Harbor Life Saving Station, built in 1897. The former harbor entrance had long since silted in, and the station had been abandoned for decades, but gradual erosion of the outer beach had brought the old building dangerously close to the surf. Last fall the Cape Cod National Seashore, in an exception to its official policy of letting nature take its course and whatever lies in it, had the station sawn in two and floated on barges twenty miles north to a safer beach at Provincetown, where it has been reassembled and turned into a museum.

It was a timely move, as it turned out, for only a few weeks later one of the most powerful ocean storms ever to hit the Cape submerged 90 percent of this beach, washing over the former site of the lifesaving station, and in the process smashing the original Tonis cottage, which had stood near it.

When I gained the beach I found the half-buried rubble of the station's foundation, and just north of it the charred remains of Tia's old family cottage, which had to be burned before they were allowed to build the new one earlier this spring. Tia blames the government for its loss, claiming that they destroyed the dune in front of the original cottage when they moved the station. "They did pile some sand back in the cut when they were through," she told me, "but no more than that. For heaven's sakes, even a child would have patted it down."

Several other cottages in the vicinity survived the storm, though the prevalence of new walls, new shingles, scattered pilings, bedsteads, and other debris in the overwash area testified that they had not escaped unscathed. A few stunted cedars, burnt orange and dead, looked planted around the houses.

The buildings all wear the aspect of a western ghost town, one that suffered some wild, violent raid, was partially rebuilt, and was then abandoned as not worth it. I am its sole inhabitant these days, but it is only the lull before the first human inundation of the season, the week before the Memorial Day weekend, when all of these beach shacks will spring back to life and hundreds of beach buggies will form a nearly continuous line of vehicles on the outer beach.

I walked back from the ocean to the bay in the sandy ruts of a vehicle trail. In the sand overwashes immediately behind the beach I found fox scat, the strong smell of skunk, and the tiny tracks of a piping plover, a small sand-colored shorebird that nests at the base of these dunes. The trail wound by some juncus bogs, bright and green and level, and passed a small brackish pond surrounded by reeds where toads call at night.

The dune cover here is almost pure beach grass, interspersed with dusty miller and new leaves of beach goldenrod. The new green blades of Ammophila are just about to overtop the dead, dry stalks of last year. There is little beach plum growing, and what there is seems about two weeks behind that on the mainland, which has already blossomed. Along the crest of the road banks are dark blue-gray tufts of poverty grass, little-rag-mop plants just beginning to green again. I stopped to stoop down and look at them, anticipating the tiny, delicate yellow flowers they would hold in June.

I felt like a farmer walking his fields, in that mixture of remembrance and anticipation between seasons. Nature is everywhere familiar in macrocosm and microcosm, in the dip and resurgence of the night-sky constellations and in the shower of green leaves welling up around old dead seed stalks. Only in the middle distance is she alien, are landscapes foreign.

III

That second night I slept a troubled sleep, a sleep of too much caffeine and germinating doubts. It rained through the night, slattering on the new asphalt roof, and through the rain and wind I heard the distant, mournful calling of the piping plover on the night beach.

As usual, following an initial, buoyant surge of self-reliance and selfish delight at having such a place all to myself, I now began to feel insufficient. Already, by Tuesday morning, I found myself thinking of my daughter's irrepressible, continual engagement with life, my father's quiet, strong, indirect love. Life is always deeper on the other side of the water, it seems, though that morning the other side remained hidden in mist and swirling fog.

The house slipped into insubstantiality as I walked down to the bay shore. I followed the dry, twisting bed of what was formerly a salt marsh creek. Now there is only a thin fringe of marsh along the western shore here. The barrier beach, gradually retreating westward in the face of the ocean's assaults, buries these tidal creeks and marshes even as it forms new ones farther west. Eventually they emerge again on the ocean side in the form of exposed peat ledges, some of which still carry the prints of old cart wheels and foraging cattle made generations ago.

The old creek bed here now fills only at high tides, the water winding cautiously, like some semi-tame animal, up to the cottage deck each morning. At ebb tide it contains a few pools, warm soupy bowls full of marsh minnows that flip about as they slowly cook.

Because of the fog I could see no birds, though I heard the chips and clicks of terns feeding in the currents offshore, and the purring, clattering hum of lobster boats laying down pots somewhere out in the bay.

I worked through the morning, writing at the large white table. Outside, the wind shifted back and forth from southeast to southwest; the fog flowed, pausing, lifting, and dropping again over the bay and the bluffs on the mainland.

I ate lunch on the deck, where tree swallows buzzed me and a trio of crows, wearing new, glistening black coats, paused briefly on the roof ridge to consider, then flew on. A horned lark landed in a bush and breasted forth a buzzy, tinkling, rising trill, one not described in the bird books. I have begun to notice that bird song, like the flowering schedule of plants, seems to be affected by the exposed environment here. The song sparrows, for instance, all have thin, scratchy, attenuated voices here, as though all the sap had been dried out of their notes by the salt air.

After lunch I took a short nap. When I woke a thin cloud cover had sucked the fog up into itself and the wind had shifted to the southwest. I painted rake trim for a few hours and then, about 4:30, walked out to the beach.

The smell of the surf, just coming in, hit me with a rich fish and salt odor, carried along on the crashing mist of its edge by a southerly breeze. I stood and inhaled it deeply, rhythmically, timing my breaths with the rush and surge of the combers.

I walked south along the undulating, ivory, grist-laced slope of the beach as the white crests caught some of the red from the sinking sun. A green glass bottle, thrown up on the sand, glinted in the reflected light. It was corked and had a message inside, written in German, which I cannot read, accompanied by several pornographic sketches—probably thrown overboard by some bored crewman not far offshore. I recorked it and threw it back into the surf, where it floated north, at about two knots.

I stopped and sat on a low dune crest pitted with ant holes and wolf-spider traps and watched the day wheel slowly down, the tide climb slowly and ponderously in. I wished I were staying for a year. I would not write for a week at a time, except to record weather, perhaps, and certain telling and vulnerable details: how the light slanted in the evening, or the taste of seaweed picked up on the beach. I would let the personal dry up or seep slowly out, regarding all inner turmoil as external, the tortuous and self-conscious processes of thought as trivial and of no account. I would let my mind be picked clean by the crows and ants and bleached by the sun, ride this thin spar of sand as it slides back and forth between the tides. I would let all feelings and their objects drift out with the daily currents and wait to see what came back ashore at the end of each week.

Walking back, I found an unfamiliar beach sparrow perched on the gable of the little outhouse. I had a sudden, fierce desire for positive identification, but I had not brought field glasses with me. *Sing, damn you, sing,* I muttered. But it only shit and flew off.

Late Tuesday afternoon the wind shifted to straight west, and now, after forty-eight hours of fog, the evening is blessedly still and clear. Only a few high, thin clouds trail among the simple stars in a rich, dark-blue sky. For the first time since arriving here I can see the mainland clear and sharp across the bay: a darkening pleat of low glacial bluffs surmounted by a line of peak-roofed houses against a red afterglow. I feel at once reattached to the world and shot with a sense of how far I have come from it. The bay waters are silky-smooth and gently undulating, but the gaily colored lobster buoys in the offshore channel reveal a strong incoming current; they strain hard at their submerged lines and lean steeply northward, sending on small wakes ahead of them.

Small flocks of plovers fly by overhead—silent, heavy-bodied forms. A pair of black-crowned night herons utter deep, guttural quawks and head south with strong, steady wingbeats to feed on the flats at the far end of the spit. Behind me, from the wet marshy hollows between the dunes, breeding Fowler's toads scream their dry, toneless screams.

The night seems to be calling me with its clarity, so in the last of the light I slip my skiff from its mooring in the creek bed, set the oars, and pull out into the current toward the straining lobster buoys. Anchoring about fifty yards out, I thrust my rubberized lantern beneath the surface and flick it on. The water is very clear and not deep, and my beam reveals its running night life. Moon jellies, with bright orange cloverleaf patterns on their domes, pulse up and down in the currents like ghostly hearts. Beneath the jellyfish are large female horseshoe crabs, ancient arthropods that resemble dark spiked shields trailing long spear points, plowing along the floor of the bay as they have for four hundred million years. Most have one smaller male, and in some cases two or three, clinging piggy-back fashion to their backs.

Drifting everywhere through the cold green waters is a fine white rain of dustlike particles. This is the phytoplankton bloom, a seasonal explosion of minute waterborne single-celled marine plants, the source of it all, the base of the estuary's rich food chain, the year's investment, bone of its body, the tiny universal foundations on which all our lives rest. Among this fine, passive dust of phytoplankton swim larger motes of zooplankton: adult copepods and arrow worms, the larval stages of crabs, barnacles, mussels, and oysters. Many of these respond positively to light; they turn and swim, jerking and twisting up toward my beam.

My light sweeps across the dark, domed forms of the submerged, lead-weighted lobster pots resting on the bottom. Inside one I sense a blurred movement and, yielding to a sudden lawless impulse, I grab its buoy line, haul it up out of some two fathoms of water, and heave it, tipping and dripping, over the gunwale of the skiff and onto the ribbed floor between my legs. Shining my light between its wooden slats and inner netting, I behold the white, ghoulish head of a large codfish spiked to the bottom of the cage for bait. The head stares up at me out of empty eye sockets, and around it dances an antic, dark collection of spider crabs, rock crabs, starfish, and one undersized lobster. The exposed creatures click, scuttle, and twist around the white fish head as though protecting their grisly treasure. I feel as though I have unearthed some undigested bit of night business.

I reach in and remove the small lobster (the owners would have to throw it back anyhow, I rationalize), then quickly heft the pot back over the side, where it sinks back down to the bottom. I row back to shore and moor my boat in the creek at the head of the tide, which to-night has almost reached the cottage. As I bolt up the steps, a splash of light from Chatham Light, two miles to the south, catches me and throws my guilty shadow up against the raw shingles like a prison searchlight. Inside, I can barely wait for the water to boil. The shell is thin. I rip the arms from the body and crunch the claws open with my teeth. To the east, beyond the dunes, beyond the mindless screaming of the toads, the night surf crawls toward its flood.

IV

I sleep a deep, dreamless sleep and wake Wednesday morning to a dawn clear but still gray. The sun, though an hour above the horizon, is in a race to overcome a rising cloud bank out over the ocean. By eight o'clock the sun wins, the bank recedes, and the morning becomes brilliant, sparkling, breezy. The bay is plied with small lobster boats, the crews checking and resetting pots. As I eat breakfast a large marsh hawk with down-swung head and upheld wings comes tilting and veering into the wind within a few yards of the west windows; it takes no more thought of this house than of a dune.

I spend the morning painting the west windows under prairie skies and rolling prairie grass, flanked by Mississippis and Missouris on all sides. The hidden surf beyond the dunes sounds like a herd of buffalo or antelope thundering down the beach, about to break through the dune hollows at any moment. The dunes themselves seem like the slick and shiny coat of some great healthy beast, muscles rippling, tumbling and galloping under my feet as I paint.

And the clouds! What a gallery of vapors there is! Tumbled cumuli pile over the mainland to the west, backed and overarched by cirrus streamers, spiderlike bursts, and paint smears. Mottled salmon clouds spread high overhead, crossed by spreading jet trails—an electron microscopy of nerve ganglions. And below these, thin, light patches of fleece race up the Outer Cape from the south.

Despite the variety of clouds, the morning remains bright. The fog, it seems, has not left for good, but has retreated north and lies, just offshore there, like some low, snarling, purplish-brown, snakelike presence— treading air, indecisive, advancing hesitantly and retreating again like some cowardly dragon, kept at bay by the offshore wind.

Painting in the lee of the house, bathing in the first good sun in three days, I lapse into the simple, expanding motions of the day. Normally I hate to paint, and might resent the time it takes away from me here. But I am doing it to help a friend who has helped me, a favor for a favor; it is only a bonus that I get to do it in such a magnificent arena. I remember, when I earned my living in a classroom, how often we all complained about the "damned mechanics" of teaching, the drudgery of it. A colleague once remarked that the touted boredom of assembly lines is only a liberal cliché, no worse than that of most jobs. But it is not drudgery or boredom per se that is unbearable, only labor or life without purpose, and no amount of bonuses, restbreaks, sabbaticals, or public recognition can make up for that. On the other hand, give us a good enough reason and we will go to hell and not resent it.

At one o'clock the fog still crouches offshore. I decide to take an after-lunch circuit walk of the south colony of cottages. The 1974 Geological Survey map shows twenty-four cottages in this group, spread out over a half-mile or so of beach. That afternoon I count twenty-two, indicating that two besides the original Tonis cottage were lost in last winter's great storm.

Beach cottage colonies tend to acquire very individual characters in different locations. Those on North Beach seem modest, middle class, and largely conventional, like the cottage owners themselves. These Chatham cottages lack the idiosyncratic elaboration of Provincetown's dune shacks, or the clustered communality of the "Village" at the tip of Barnstable's Sandy Neck. They are, instead, simple, restrained, and solid (or as solid as beach shacks can be), placed two to three hundred feet apart, as though seeking neither solitude nor true society, but comfortable association, seeking to be with but not of their own kind—not unlike certain nesting seabirds. They represent a kind of pared-down, unlandscaped counterpart to the settled, bourgeois character of the mainland community, an escape from some of the latter's specific restraints, the sharp edges and binding fabrics of communal living, without losing its basic forms. So our outriders are still characteristic of the main mountain ranges.

The owners these days tend to be from neighboring Cape towns like Dennis and Brewster, but some name signs I encounter are pure Chatham still: Nickerson and Lumpkin on my nearest neighbor's, Crowell on a beached boat.

Inside, most of these cottages are plain, even negligently spartan. Some have imported trappings of suburban rec rooms: masonite paneling, captain's chairs, coasters, "Old Philosopher" wall paintings, et cetera. But outside, all retain an enforced simplicity, a perpetually nomadic look, like dice thrown and rethrown again on the gaming table of the beach. There is little of that external, self-conscious, quaint cuteness that infects so much of the mainland's dwellings, from lobster pots on the lawns to hawser-and-pier fencing to "Cod's Little

Acre" and "Our Hide-Aweigh" carved quarterboards over the garages. What there is of this is relegated mostly to the outhouses, perennial source of amusement among refugees from indoor plumbing. One has a "Lobster Potty II" sign above its door, with a genuine wooden pot mounted on the roof. The few signs attached to the cottages themselves tend to be self-deprecating—"Nauset Hilton" on a boathouse—or bristly—"Warning: Trap Gun Set" on a boarded-up window.

There is a kind of landscape humor to them as well. Their owners seem to enjoy bringing in useless artifacts of civilization and planting them around their houses: fire hydrants, newspaper boxes, "Keep Off the Grass" signs. It is a kind of inverse boasting, a reveling in their temporary freedom from the tyranny of what these objects symbolize. One owner has nailed an electric meter to the side of a wall.

I know the freedom from civilized discontent that these cottages celebrate, for I have something of a previous history in one of them. During summers in college I worked as a counselor at one of the Cape sailing camps a few miles north of here on the mainland. On occasion we took a whaleboat full of boys across the bay for an overnight stay in the camp-owned "Outer Beach Cabin." These trips were always sparked with a spirit of adventure and lawlessness. Distinctions between counselor and camper tended to break down, and sometimes we aided the boys in the officially proscribed nighttime activity of digging beach buggy traps. These were deep holes dug in existing vehicle tracks on the outer beach designed to catch unsuspecting fishermen or campers. After finishing a trap, we hid behind a dune, waiting for a pair of headlights to come bouncing down the beach, watching as one of the lights suddenly dropped at an angle, and stifling conspiratorial laughter as a volley of oaths erupted from the invisible driver.

I wonder about the origins of these colonies. Why did they cluster just where they did, a couple of dozen here, another twenty a half-mile to the north, and nothing in between? Most of the buildings appear to have been built after World War II. I have an older map, surveyed in 1940, which shows only seven structures on the entire beach. The cottages in each colony are connected to one another by a complex series of trails threading through a maze of wet swales full of bayberry, beach rose, poison ivy, and wild cranberry.

It would be fun, given the time and opportunity, to study the social organization of such informal multi-generational beach communities, to chronicle the connections, civilities, folklore, and customs that have grown up in them. There must, I think, be conflicting tendencies toward privacy and intercourse in a setting so open and impressionable. Already I can discern a light but definite path running along the top of the dune ridge between the new Tonis cottage and the one immediately south. But I am just as glad to have the neighborhood to myself this time, not to have to get to know people as well as their dwellings. One set of neighbors at a time.

v

Sometime during the night the fog returned, blanketing the house again. I wake and feel islanded in its midst, like some cloudy, dilating eye unable to focus. I open the door and listen to the thin, high, attenuated calls of the birds of this outer land: the twinkling, metallic cries of the least terns, scratchy notes of song sparrows, chips of savannah sparrows, rising tinkles of larks, old-man coughs of black-beaked gulls, strident cackles of laughing gulls.

By midmorning a light spitting rain begins; it lifts the fog some but drives all boats on the bay to shelter. The gulls, unperturbed, promenade like burgomeisters on the bars in front of the cottage. The rain hits the asphalt roof with a pliant softness, gurgles down off the eaves.

I try to write, but it is no go. It is hard writing about the life one is actually living. I came out here in part to put some distance between it and me, but I find I carry it around with me, unfinished. Thoreau wrote about Walden mostly after leaving it. The best accounts are always separate finished episodes—Melville at sea, Whitman in the first flush of self-discovery, Hemingway at war—rather than the impossibly disparate grist of one's current daily existence. In such situations short, quick raids seem to be best: a day on the beach, a week in the garden, an hour on the road. Beyond that there is too much life to order, to give shape and meaning to. One never seems to get to the end of it.

It rains all afternoon, heavy at times. The air has turned soft and heavy. I paint screen doors inside, and for the first time I miss not having a radio. What I miss most is music. Thoreau took his flute to the pond. Henry Beston brought his concertina to the Outermost House. I play piano.

By evening my schedule has crumbled away completely. No painting. A cold dinner. I prowl the empty neighborhood for novelty and find, in one of the open outhouses, two old copies of *Playboy* from 1966, its heyday. So innocent and positive they seem now, so *therapeutic* about sex. Having largely succeeded in what it set out to do, the magazine now seems forced to do more than it wants to, to appease the endless craving for novelty and the forbidden that it helped to legitimize.

Oh, we are all such horrible mixtures. It is amazing that anything clean and simple ever comes out of any of us. Any writer's honest journal is at once a revelation and an enigma.

VI

Friday. The holiday weekend begins with yet another morning of general fog, southeasterly wind, and spattering rain. Gulls perch like hungry senators at the edge of visibility. Terns call invisibly out of the gray. The southeast corner of the house soughs with surf, and the marsh hawk tilts over the bending, wind-stirred grass like some great brown and white butterfly.

South-southeast! It is as though someone opened a quadrant of the globe and forgot to close it, letting loose the unending, rearing tides of wind and fog. There is no bird song anywhere this morning. Even the terns seem quieted by the monolithic persistence of this weather. The fog is a great gray god, a silent river like the flowing plankton borne ceaselessly along by the channel currents, impregnating the bay.

South-southeast! Flow on, moon jellies, flow on, plankton! The lobster buoys strain at their lines, leaning desirously northward, throwing their wakes ahead of them, held by the weighted, slatted traps on the sea bottom where claws, horny shells, and disked feet dance, click, and scuttle around eyeless, spiked fish heads. The circus-colored buoys bend like the dune grass in the wind, flying ceaselessly but going nowhere. I would fly away, too, now, but am held down here by lead weights and dead lures of resolution and commitment. I feel like a barnacle or a spirobus worm anchored to this house, throwing out feathered legs and tentacles of myself, then withdrawing to digest my finds.

Late in the morning the first campers of the weekend begin to lumber down the beach, fog or no fog. The rain stops by noon, and I spend most of the afternoon painting trim and windows on the north side. The fog lifts enough so that through my glasses I can see a small-craft warning flag flying from the Coast Guard station next to Chatham Light. I think about rowing across tonight to see a movie, maybe calling home. . . . But the wind picks up till there are whitecaps on the bay, and by dusk the fog has closed in again, shutting out the shore lights, keeping me honest.

It is after eleven at night now. Beyond the dunes the surf is rising, its imperative thumping penetrating the thin walls of this uninsulated house. It has been a make-work, make-play day, and I feel both enervated and restless. Placing a Coleman lantern in the east window as a beacon, I set out across the dunes to the ocean. I walk southeast, oblique to the shore, following the sound of the surf. Sights and sounds are both muffled in the darkness and fog. Chatham Light is only an obscure, intermittent glow off to my right. Offshore the deep bleating of two ship horns far apart carries like the baying of two great sea beasts in the night. Toads breed, screaming at one another in the wet hollows.

I seem to be traveling in a dim world of homogenized senses, where distance and dimension cease to exist. For an indeterminate time I walk without seeming to get any nearer the sound of the surf, then all at once I smell it, a wall of sea odors immediately ahead—rich, salt-spiced, redolent of fecundity and decay.

The tide is approaching its high. The seethe of incoming foam laps and sloshes just below the wrack line on the upper beach, sliding back toward the dark breakers with a bubbly, sucking withdrawal. The breaking crest of the waves and the foamy swash edge appear to be outlined with a faint phosphorescence, but it is hard to tell in the obscurity of the fog. The wrack line itself—a knotted tangle of rockweed, dulse, mermaid's tresses, broken claws and shells—is speckled with thousands of tiny, pale, yellow-green coals of light. This is bioluminescent plankton, hordes of diatoms, dinoflagellates and copepods that in summer fill vast stretches of the ocean with their cold, chemical glow—a sort of *aurora maritima*—so that ships plowing through these living shoals of light leave wide wakes of flickering fire behind them.

Some of the larger glowing particles in the wrack line are hopping about, like sparks from resinous kindling. Shining my flashlight on them, I see the bouncing forms of sand hoppers, or beach fleas—miniature, shrimplike crustaceans about a third of an inch long, with huge eyes and pearly-white bodies. By day they live in burrows on the upper beach, coming out at night to feed on the tide's leavings. They ingest the tiny phosphorescent plankton, and their semitransparent bodies begin to glow like miniature jars full of fireflies.

The ocean shows no inordinate ambition tonight, staying contained for the most part, in orderly restlessness, within the high, steep berm of its own making, content to spit up these luminous bits of life. Yet now a larger wave than usual breaks, invisibly, far out; its grating roar seems to spread and encircle me, the dark beach loses definition and place, and though its seethe only curls up and licks my boots like a puppy, I feel a rush of vertigo beneath me, shiver deeply, and involuntarily step back. Vulnerable of spirit, I seem no more than one of those pale, glowing specks of moribund animal life in the wrack line before me, invisible except for the cold, weak light I give off, lasting a few moments, then going out forever.

Now there are other lights moving on the beach. A trio of beach buggies loom out of the fog from the north, their headlight beams lurching drunkenly over the inner sand trail behind the dunes. As they pass the cut where I stand, I can make out fishing poles erect in quivers mounted to their front bumpers. One tries to cut out to the beach over a dune, fails, and roars back onto the track. A man in another jeep curses loudly in the darkness as he passes. For a moment I think he is shouting at me, but then a woman's crackly voice, unangry, bantering, answers him unintelligibly on his CB radio.

They pass swiftly, their lights disappearing into the fog before them, and where they have been I hear the lovely, mournful, solitary note of the piping plover.

For once I do not resent the intrusions of these machines on our beaches, their meaningless lights and harsh sounds. I understand what draws them out here and feel a strong urge to follow them down the dark strand, down past the last of the cottages to the far tip of the spit where the sands perpetually shift and the night herons feed, where men cast their hooks into the curved breakers and pull living, flapping, cold fish-flesh out of the side of the sea.

We all have a desire to seek out such primal encounters, however clumsily or blindly. And the relentless complexity and growing numbers of our society seem to force us to seek them at ever odder hours and in ever stranger places, as on this exposed and shrouded beach, flooded and freshened by the night.

VII

Saturday. Last night I dreamed that I was riding down North Beach in the company of clowns on unicycles. We kept avoiding holes that had been dug in the sand, laughing and singing as we went. Eventually we came to what seemed to be a small tourist or information center, somewhere south of this cottage. It had a makeshift telephone system, and I tried to call home but was frustrated by operators too friendly and chatty to bother placing my call, phones with complicated and obscure dialing instructions, intermittent connections with the mainland that seemed to be dependent on the tides. There was one strange phone that had been jury-rigged from old washing-machine parts and that kept agitating on me as I tried to use it. I guess I am ready to go home.

But there will be no going over this morning. I woke at 5:30 to heavy rain, fog, and strong southwest winds. After breakfast it cleared somewhat, but has closed down again and the fog has been dense ever since. Nonetheless the holiday clammers and beachcombers continue to arrive, replacing the shorebirds and terns on the bars and flats in front of the cottage. I have cleaned up and packed, will paint some more inside, and will try to go over after lunch.

At noon the fog finally lifts. Leaving the heavy gear again for Tia, who will arrive that afternoon, I row across, touching the mainland at about two o'clock. I walk the boat upcurrent along the shore of Tern Island to the Chatham Fish Pier. Rows of patterned plover heads follow me above the tall, bright-green juncus grass of the inner marshes, and a large flock of mixed gulls sit along the southern dunes, unfazed as always.

I haul the boat out beside the pier, with the strange sense of landing on a foreign shore, realizing that I have spoken to no human being for nearly a week, wondering if I still know the language. I call Beth at work—my voice works, she seems to recognize me—but she can't pick me up for another two hours. So I decide to walk into Chatham Center, to reacquaint myself with civilization.

I set off along Seaview Street, carrying my backpack and drinking a Coke. I am grungy and my clothes are dirty and wrinkled, but I feel strangely elated and unselfconscious. As I walk I become gradually aware of and infused by sounds and sights I seem to remember as if from childhood: the smooth hum of lawnmowers, the full-throated song of a song sparrow, hedges, robins. A woman in white golf clothes swings at a ball on the public course, misses, swings again, and hits it about eight feet—some strange native ritual, no doubt. And there are unexpected patterns of wires overhead, and pavement under my feet, and children playing and fighting on front porches, and tourists walking along Main Street, arms around one another, and the smell of cut flowers from florist shops, and the sight of women with done hair and clean blouses stiting on high stools inside ice-cream shops—I want to go in and buy them something.

There are cars, of course—but it is not the sight of cars that touches me, not car noises and car smells, not the fast food and motel strips, not any of the harsh contrasts of civilization that my mind has unconsciously set up defenses against, but rather these easy motions and simple signs of our occupation of the earth.

Chatham, with its long-settled, well-cared-for look, its easy access to wider horizons—where the Atlantic lies literally at the end of Main Street—is probably one of the best ports of reentry into the human world. The afternoon is a kind of decompression chamber for me, leaving the marvelous and dreadful vacuum of the outer beach, moving away from that intense, consuming pressure of self-consciousness, expanding in the sunlit crowds.

I walk along, soaking up the sights, giving myself over to the human currents that are just beginning to fill the sidewalks and the shops. I walk into a florist shop and buy blue cornflowers for Beth, buy some small toys for the kids in the five-and-ten, and carry the packages around proudly like badges of readmittance. Everyone seems so helpful and pleasant. I have forgotten the simple but deep pleasure of being waited on courteously by a store clerk or a waitress. I play willingly the role of tourist and consumer, talking with people I would not normally speak to, just to hear the sound of their voices, the varieties of timbre and accent. It seems amazing that I can get people to speak to me just by speaking to them. It is as though I had at last mastered birdcalls.

I had expected to feel a certain letdown upon returning, but the effect is just the opposite. Somehow the fact of human existence strikes me as miraculous, as though never seen clearly before. I feel a little like Emily in *Our Town*, returning to earth for one day after her death, as a child. I want to cry out to those I pass and who pass me the simple wonder of us all being here together in this lovely place under sky and shade and sun-dappled yards and the song of birds. I know that inevitably I will

sink back into the dulling effects of routine, into posses-
siveness, into trivial irritation, into the short-sighted
pursuits that hobble and frustrate so much of our short
lives. But for a few hours I am granted a fresh look at
what I have left, which, if not, as T. S. Eliot claimed,
the sole point of all our journeying, is reward enough.

It is a little after four now, and I am back at the fish pier,
standing on the loading platform, waiting for my family.
Less than a mile across Pleasant Bay, the cottage where
I lived alone for a week sits clear and gray now under
the first sun in three days. It seems so close, and yet
years away, across the gleaming boat-plied waters. Below me crews in yellow rubber aprons fork the gutted
flapping carcasses of codfish from their boat decks into
a large metal hopper. When the hopper is full it is raised
by a hydraulic winch and dumps its load, letting go a
cascade of bloody disemboweled fish that goes sliding
down a white ramp into the icy-breath'd hold of the
packing plant. Though most of the fish will be shipped
off to New York or Boston in huge refrigerated trucks,
and though whole striped bass now sells for more than
prime rib in the public fish market next door, we can
still see the elemental processes of our survival in such
places as this.

A young man on the dock calls to a friend who is just
getting into a new green Toyota with a Connecticut
license plate: "Those Canadian girls, they going to be
back this summer?" The friend smiles, raises his thumb,
and drives off. I smile too, content to be where I am,
standing in this place of migrations and appetites, listening to the endless talk of fish, weather, and the chances
of love.

Sea St.

THE STREET SIGN is still there, the old-fashioned wooden kind with black letters on a white background: SEA ST. Occasionally a car will turn down the street, perhaps a former East Dennis resident attempting to return for a visit, perhaps a tourist trying to find a bay beach, lured by the name on the sign. But after a few moments the car backs out onto Route 6A again and, puzzled or frustrated, continues on down the highway.

Though Sea Street is still listed as a functioning thoroughfare on most current Cape Cod road maps, and a double yellow line still runs incongruously down the middle of its asphalt, you do not have to travel more than a few yards down the street before you realize that this road is closed. Now, in all their lush, high-summer profusion, the honeysuckle, chokecherry, sumac, blackberries, viburnum, and other roadside shrubs and vines billow out from either side of the road like green waves about to close in again on some impudent parting of their sea. And if you persist and push your vehicle through the foliage-constricted passage to emerge onto a relatively wide portion of blacktop, you realize that further travel, if any, will have to be on foot.

Sea Street is an old road, well over a hundred years old, and until some nine years ago it served to connect Quivett Neck in East Dennis with Route 6A in West Brewster. Quivett Neck is technically a marsh island, and the construction of Sea Street must have been a major engineering feat in its day, requiring as it did the building of an earth causeway across some two hundred yards of salt marsh. A culvert was maintained beneath the causeway, but the tidal flow was severely restricted, and the marsh on the upper or western side of the road is now a mixture of freshwater, brackish, and saltwater vegetation: marsh elder, cattail, bayberry, winterberry, phragmites reed, salt hay, and, surprisingly, several red cedars.

In time, as the East Dennis community grew, several homes were built along the edge of this upper marsh, protected from severe flooding during northeast storms by the road dike. Nonetheless, during certain high course tides and storm surges, the causeway would be over-washed, and periodically Sea Street would have to be repaired or reconstructed, a cost borne jointly by the two towns.

One does not often see a town-owned road fall into disuse anymore, especially when it connects two towns together. In this case, however, it was precisely Sea Street's joint ownership by Brewster and Dennis that led to its abandonment. About a decade ago, when the road once again needed major maintenance, the town of Brewster balked at bearing its share of the cost. Perhaps it was due to the skyrocketing costs of road repair and asphalt in recent years, or to the lessening of historic ties between the East Dennis and West Brewster communities. Whatever the reasons, Brewster refused to budge and finally voted at its annual town meeting to officially close the road.

Some Brewster residents felt that the asphalt and causeway should be removed entirely, allowing the upper marsh to revert to salt marsh. But it was feared by others that the heavy machinery required to do this might cause more harm than benefit to the marsh. Also, the marsh edge residents in East Dennis, worried that if the dike were removed their septic systems and basements might be flooded, threatened to sue. The idea was squelched, the road was neither repaired nor removed, and by default nature was left to take its own course.

It has done so, with a beautiful vengeance. When the road was closed, yellow-painted concrete barriers were erected at either end at the beginning of the causeway. The barrier on the Brewster side, about two hundred feet in from Route 6A, is almost completely smothered by grape and poison ivy vines, which have used it as a trellis. A narrow gap was left in the barriers to allow continued bicycle and foot traffic. For several years not much change occurred out on the dike. A weed or two grew up from cracks in the asphalt. Dried marsh grass, washed up by storm tides, was left to rot on the pavement, eventually forming a thin humus.

But in the last couple of years the deterioration has accelerated dramatically. It has become unsafe to ride a bicycle across. The asphalt has collapsed in large sinkholes in several places, with seaside goldenrod sprouting up out of their bottoms. Vines have grown out across the road surface, and roadside wildflowers, such as Queen Anne's lace, bristly rose, bouncing bet, spurge, wild pinks, beach pea, and numerous others are fast becoming road flowers.

Even more dramatically, the pavement itself has been riddled by underground runners of phragmites and beach grass, whose stalks have burst up through the pavement, perforating its surface and rapidly breaking it apart. In places the hydraulic jackhammering advance of these plants has progressed from both sides toward the middle so that they are now only a few feet apart, like transcontinental railroad lines about to meet.

There has, curiously, been one human improvement to this road since it was officially closed. Two years ago the Dennis Highway Department installed a new thirty-inch culvert beneath the dike at the town line in an attempt to increase the herring run into Mud Pond above the marsh. Though some marsh edge residents again voiced fears of flooding, the larger culvert was installed and the run appears to be flourishing. In this one instance, at least, passage of fish seems to have outlasted passage of people.

I am not sure what has moved me to write about this road, and even less sure about how I feel, finally, about its imminent disappearance. Sea Street is, as much as any in the area, an historic road. It is storied, and represents human ties that crossed town boundaries. It reflects its name, Sea Street, so well, providing a magnificent view of the marsh and the bay beyond to anyone who crosses it. The town line sign, rusted and leaning now over the bank of Quivett Creek, is a reminder of how many *inland* boundaries of our towns are determined by water in one form or another.

I realize that, by going a few hundred feet farther west along Route 6A, I will still be able to walk, bike, or drive into East Dennis, so that the loss of the road will be a very minor inconvenience. Yet somehow it was more fitting to cross this old marsh road. It represented a time crossing as well, into one of the older Cape villages, where as recently as a generation ago most of the families living there shared the same last name. Nate Black the barber, who lived on my road in West Brewster, crossed Sea Street on foot for decades two evenings a week to give haircuts in the basement of David H. Sears's store, and many East Dennis residents came by the same road to get their corn meal or spring herring at Stony Brook.

In principle I was and still am for removing the road and dike entirely and allowing the upper marsh to revert to salt marsh. Conservationists, I guess, do not have much sympathy for property values, at least for those in another town. Yet in fact I have some reservations about the idea. I am not so much concerned about flooded basements that may result from such action as I am about, say, a few stands of uncommon cardinal flowers, whose slender spikes of intense scarlet flowers blossom in late summer in a few hidden pockets of the upper marsh. At the extreme western end of the marsh is the only known stand of European black alder, *Alnus glutinosa*, on Cape Cod. This tree is an alien species, and no one seems to know how it got there, but the existence of the grove may be endangered if the dike is removed.

Should these things be environmental considerations? At what point do we say that an environment has adapted to man-made changes and produced an integrated community with as much validity as the original one? We are just learning how certain "natural" landscapes, such as the Nantucket moors or the Provincetown dunes, are dependent on human alteration for their continued existence. I suppose that what should be done is what in all probability will be done—that is, nothing—and that eventually, gradually, the dike will be breached for good.

But my mixed feelings about the road's fate go beyond such environmental considerations. I myself voted to close the road, partially for reasons that had little to do with ecological or economic issues. I almost always vote against new roads at town meetings. I root for potholes, applaud frost heaves, and cheer for curves. And in this case I was pleased that, in an age of metastasizing highways, at least one vehicular corridor had been cut off, amputated.

Yet I felt a light regret as the road became progressively unsafe to ride bikes across. And now that my days of pedestrian passage seem limited, I begin to have serious second thoughts. Shouldn't some passage be maintained? Perhaps a raised wooden walkway could be constructed that would allow full tidal passage beneath it, thus providing the best of both worlds? But that, I know, would also have to be a joint town project, and an expensive one. Would those Dennis drivers whose wishes we snubbed a few years ago be willing to support Brewster pedestrians now?

I suppose what it comes down to is this: at some point, no matter how much we love wilderness, we begin to regret, if not resent, the disappearance of any human passage. For a while it may please us to behold nature reclaiming what presumptuous man has opened up, bridged over, or filled in. But if the passage gets too restricted, or threatens to go completely, we are suddenly reminded of our race's vulnerability, of our hard-won clearings on this continent, and of nature's readiness to swallow us back up. We find ourselves, against our better principles, beginning to take sides with those who should have known better than to build so close to the edge of a marsh, or on land that will be gone beneath the waves in a hundred centuries or so, or on a planet that, at best, has only a few million more millennia to breathe.

The Sands of Monomoy

I HAVE BEEN BURNED. I sit here in the cool
morning shade of our oaks and I can feel my face
burning, radiating the heat of yesterday's sun, sun that
glinted off emerald swells, bone- and shell-strewn sands,
silvered flats. Was it only yesterday I was there? It
seems a thousand days away. Yet last night in my sleep
I still felt the rocking of the waters beneath me, heard
and saw the rush and rise of ten thousand wings before
me, and drank in the clean tide of solitude that rolled
over the flats, across the rippling expanses of marsh
grass, the hidden, salty ponds, and the hollows and
gentle rises of the dune battlements.

I feel a lump in the pocket of my jeans, reach down,
and pull out a handful of sand. It is not ordinary Cape
Cod sand, but an extremely fine variety, twice-sifted,
water-milled, and wind-distilled. There are over a thousand grains to the square centimeter. They roll and flow

into the veins of my palm almost like water, like diamond dust. They are the sands of Monomoy.

Monomoy Island drops off the chin of Chatham like the beard of the Cape, the barbel of its Cod-fish. Like beards and barbels it is an outgrowth of the main body, though at the moment a disconnected one. A product of wind and sea, it is composed of glacial material worn from the cliffs of the Outer Beach to the north, carried southward by strong longshore currents, and deposited below Pleasant Bay, first as an underwater bar, then as exposed shoals, and finally as an eight-mile barrier island of low sand dunes, sculptured by the wind and held tenuously stable by beach grass.

If Cape Cod is a metaphor for time, a constantly changing land form registering the geological hours, then Monomoy Island is its sweep second hand, caught in the grip of the same forces of change, but recording them much more quickly and visibly. It is the cartographer's despair and the coastal geologist's delight.

Seen from the air, the long, thin island appears as some giant seabird, soaring seaward out of Nantucket Sound, its great wings feathered out into the marshes and flats to the west. Seen in time-lapse photography, it would appear to form the southern end of a twenty-mile whip of barrier beaches and barrier islands lashing the inner coast of Chatham, dissolving and re-forming over and over again through the centuries.

There is something about the nature of Monomoy that invites metaphor, as though with enough images we might somehow shackle its shifting, protean shape. It seems, in its constant mutations, an image itself, illusory, ephemeral; yet it is as rooted in reality as the Rockies, and its changes merely attest to the intensity of its existence.

I had for several years wanted to visit Monomoy. From the mainland portion of the Monomoy National Wildlife Refuge it looms across the channel, teasingly close, like a floating mirage, like Oz, white and green. There are Audubon trips and other groups that go regularly to the island by charter boat, but it seemed to me to be one of those natural presences that ask, initially at least, to be encountered alone, unguided, to see what it has to offer.

And so yesterday I borrowed a canoe and set off from the Morris Island Dike, paddling down through the narrow outlet of Pleasant Bay toward Monomoy's northern tip. It was a beautiful August day of premature fall weather, cool, with a light breeze out of the northeast and white sprays of high cirrus clouds spouting up to the south over the island.

I rode rapidly down its ocean-facing shore, riding with the tide on clear, heaving swells. I was surprised at how gentle these sea swells remained, but the long curving tip of North Beach to the east still extended itself like a shield, and beyond that, farther south, the rush and clash of whitecaps indicated the presence of the Monomoy shoals. These bars and shoals have threatened and claimed hundreds of ships ever since the early French explorers named it Cape Malabarre—"Cape of the Evil Bars"—but today they offered protection to me and to Monomoy itself.

I first made a landing about a half-mile down the outside shore, and was almost immediately assaulted by hordes of biting greenhead flies, which breed abundantly in the nearby marshes. Wildlife on Monomoy is not "managed," not even the flies. The wooden greenhead-fly trap boxes so common on the mainland are missing in these marshes, and the visitor without long clothes and insect repellent comes here in August at his peril.

Just inside the dunes at this point is the Monomoy tern colony, the largest in the state, posted and patrolled by the Massachusetts Audubon Society. During the past breeding season some two thousand common, several hundred roseate, a few dozen least, and a handful of arctic terns nested here. Largely protected from human disturbance, the terns of Monomoy are, according to Audubon tern warden Peter Trull, "barely holding their own" against beach erosion, encroaching herring gulls, and natural predators such as owls and night herons. Their numbers, in fact, have been slipping gradually but steadily in recent years.

When I arrived, in mid-August, breeding had been over for several weeks and the posted signs had been removed. The arctic terns had long departed, having the farthest to travel, and while many birds could still be seen on the island, they no longer hovered and screamed over their nests.

Now, in late summer, the colony had a strange, deserted look. I walked down through the hollows between the dunes, out onto a kind of flattened alley, a pathway of some former flood tide. Its floor was laced with lovely lavender mats of seaside spurge. Here and there among the spurge I came upon the remains of nests and, occasionally, pairs of mottled greenish-beige eggs encircled, as though by the tide, with bits of marsh grass and blackened seaweed. Most were abandoned, but some were still warm, a second clutch probably, still being incubated by a few of the adults, but standing almost no

chance at this late date of hatching and fledging before
the parents deserted them. Under one of these egg-filled
nests I saw, protruding from the sand, the skull of a
night heron, blown white and clean by the abrading
wind.

To the west of the colony spread the broad green
expanse of salt marsh and the beginning of the tidal mud
flats. Here many of the terns were resting, the young
fledged common terns easily distinguished at close range
by their darker plumage, white foreheads, black bills,
and prominent black wingbars. There were also several
"peep"—small sandpipers, sanderlings, and plovers—
running and poking about in the mud and the undrained
tidal creeks. But here, on the island's backside, the tide
was still a half-mile or more out, and most of the thousands of migrating shorebirds that congregate on Monomoy in late summer and early fall would not be visible
for several hours yet.

I returned to the canoe on the ocean side and set off
again, paddling toward Hammond's Bend, the narrowest
point of the island, about two miles farther south. There
I planned to portage across, explore the area to the south
on foot, and paddle back on the Sound side in the afternoon in time to catch the shorebirds.

Paddling south on the outside of Monomoy is a curious
and tricky business. The farther one goes, the more one
emerges from the protection of the shoals and bars to
the east. Although the swells themselves were still
relatively gentle, they began to break higher and higher
as I continued down the beach. I started to wonder if I
could make a landing at Hammond's Bend without
capsizing.

But the landing proved easier than I had anticipated.
Working my way carefully in, I was lifted by a swell and

deposited as carefully as a plover's egg on the beach. Before I could pull the canoe out of the surf's reach, however, a second wave came in and swamped the stern. No farther by boat, it seemed to say. Foot it from here.

II

I dragged the canoe onto the upper beach. The isthmus at Hammond's Bend was barely a hundred yards wide, and drift lines from high tides on either side came within half that distance of each other.* Shouldering a small pack, I crossed the narrow waist and set off along the long inner curve of Hammond's Bend to explore the older southern portion of the island. Except for a large splotch of tidal flats off Inward Point, the shallows and marshes south of this bight are much narrower than those of the northern end. It makes for fewer greenhead flies, but also for fewer shorebirds. This is more than made up for, however, by a much greater variety of terrain, including a number of small brackish ponds, higher dunes, shrub forests containing Monomoy's elusive but sizable deer herd, and patches of the largest, sweetest blackberries I've ever tasted.

At Inward Point there was the remnant of a colony of old beach shacks—small, indigenous, eccentric wooden structures with whimsical names like Tinkerbell School and Whelk-um—slipped between dune hollows or perched on slender sand pillars as though on stilts. I

---

* Six months after my visit here, on February 7, 1978, a massive ocean storm breached this isthmus, separating the upper third of the island from the rest. It remains today as a wide, open channel through which small boats may pass at high tide.

investigated one that looked empty, a low-built shack with a junkyard of mattresses and other debris scattered outside. Dozens of migrating barn swallows perched and soared about it, celebrating the discovery of a human-built oasis in this structural desert, and giving it at once an air of domesticity and abandonment. At least it looked abandoned, but when I peered through one of the loose windows I saw a wet washcloth hung up to dry and a clock on a small table, ticking loudly away.

I counted only three cottages at Hammond's Bend, in an area where my 1964 Geological Survey Map showed nine. These buildings are part of a vanishing species, doomed by Congress in 1970 by the designation of Monomoy as part of the National Wilderness Preservation system (the only official wilderness in Massachusetts and one of the few on the entire East Coast). Except in this handful of preexisting buildings, no overnight camping is allowed on the island, and even these cottages will gradually be eliminated as tenancy agreements with the U.S. Fish and Wildlife Service expire or, as seems more likely, the ocean swallows them first.

As such, these few remaining cottages represent the last act in a long drama of human use and occupation of Monomoy. As early as 1711 an intrepid settler came here and opened a tavern at Wreck Cove, a former harbor just south of these cottages. In those days the island, then attached to the mainland, served as common pasture for the Chatham townspeople, and the "Common Flats" were harvested for salt hay. In the 1820s Monomoy Light was built at the south end near Monomoy Point, and during the mid-nineteenth century a good-sized fishing community, known as Whitewash Village, flourished west of Monomoy Point around a deep harbor, complete with stores, a tavern, and a school.

In its time the sands of Monomoy have also harbored four lifesaving stations, a Coast Guard station, hunting clubs, and summer cottages. Of all man's many footholds on the island, only the abandoned lighthouse tower, the Coast Guard boathouse, and a handful of summer camps remain. Nothing more, by law, may be built.

I took lunch in the shade of one of the shacks near the beach and then, rolling up my pants, forded Train's Creek, a wide tidal stream connected to a large stretch of ditched inland marsh and a shallow brackish impoundment known as Hospital Pond. This marsh system and the pond are all that is left of the old Wreck Cove. I do not know how Hospital Pond got its intriguing name, but a possible source is an incident that occurred during the winter of 1729 when the *George and Ann*, sailing from Dublin with a shipload of emigrants, took refuge there. Storms, disease, overcrowding, and a lack of provisions had already claimed over one hundred lives and brought the survivors close to mutiny when they were spotted by a Captain Lothrop and led to harbor in Wreck Cove. The passengers and crew spent the winter boarding with the village families, receiving both hospital care and hospitality, and finally resumed their voyage in the spring.

South of Train's Creek I came upon a graveyard of shells—large sea scallops, knobbed and waved whelks, moon snails—a sea chest of delicate, sculptured, pastel forms. There were hundreds of them, lying in dense concentrations and windrows as though carried in by some previous flood tide and deposited in piles, crowning the low sand hills with fans and whorls of purple, yellow, and orange shells.

Beyond the shell piles was a stretch of small barren sand bowls where the island's numerous gulls apparently came to congregate, and to die. Their gray mummified bodies were stretched indecorously about, legs up, and here and there a whitened bone thrust up through the sand. I came upon one carcass that looked recently dead and experimentally pushed on its diaphragm; it uttered a series of soft, hoarse honks, like a rusty harmonium.

III

The felicities of political language, which flowered in the early days of the Republic in the noble phrases of declarations, constitutions, and judicial decisions, seem in our time to survive, when they survive at all, largely in legislation relating to the preservation of natural areas. Public Law 88-577 of 1964, better known as the Wilderness Act, provides one of the few contemporary examples. It contains the terms under which Monomoy Island was established as a Wilderness Area: "an area where the earth and its community of life are untrammeled by man, where man himself is a visitor who does not remain."

As I walked down and across the rims and bowls of the sand hollows south of Train's Creek, the fittingness of these words seemed to spread all about me. Here was life and death in untrammeled freedom; here were the skulls of herons supporting tern eggs, mollusk shells building their own lovely monuments atop sand knolls, gull corpses singing their own dirges, and weathered shacks, wreathed with swallows, sinking gracefully toward oblivion.

"Untrammeled"—what a marvelous word! Commonly confused with "untrampled," it has a very different meaning, namely, "unrestricted in activity or free movement."

It derives from "trammel," a shackle attached to a horse's leg to teach it the artificial gait of ambling. Here on Monomoy, at least, nothing was forced to march at an unnatural pace.

I crossed east from the Sound shore over some low dune ridges to Hospital Pond. On the far side of the pond were half a dozen large white egrets, four snowies and two common, standing still as cardboard cutouts on stalked legs in the shallow water. As I squatted down to watch them, something rustled in the marsh grass nearby. I rose up slightly and saw a movement of mottled gray and white among the dark green blades: a juvenile herring gull, probably unfledged and hiding.

I did not want to disturb the egrets by flushing it, but all at once the bird flapped jerkily out of the grass and onto the pond into view. Something was horribly wrong with it. Its neck was twisted, bent backward and down to one side nearly into the water. It seemed to have no control over its movements and began to drift away from me in the slight breeze toward the far side of the pond.

I shed my pack, stripped off my clothes, and plunged with a loud splash into the shallow, lukewarm water. The egrets, startled, rose with hoarse croaks and broad, slow wingbeats, while hordes of marsh minnows spread out in waves before me. In a few strokes I caught up with the crippled gull and discovered its plight. It had become hooked by a fishing lure that had probably washed up with the tide. One of the lure's three hooks had pierced the bird's left knee joint and another was jammed into its left nostril, bending the bird nearly double.

I stood up in the shallow water and clasped its body to me with one arm while I removed the hook in its knee with my other hand. The gull, with a wild stoicism and weakened resistance, kept its beak clamped shut, but I managed to pry it open and free the second hook. When I looked in its mouth I thought at first that its tongue had been ripped, but on closer inspection I realized that a gull's tongue is curiously detached and serrated at its rear end.

I released the bird and watched it float across the pond to the far bank, where it limped ashore, fluttered in the air a few yards, and came to a wobbly landing on its injured leg.

I waded back to the near shore, shivering for several minutes as the sun dried me off, and put my clothes back on. However Hospital Pond had gotten its name, I had no illusions about its efficacy in this case. There was a good chance the gull would die of gangrene from the rusted hooks, but surely it would have died a painful and hobbled death by starvation if I had not come upon it, a fate no creature deserves.

Shouldering my pack, I once more headed south. Why had the bird's plight affected me so much? Surely nature is capable of equally pitiless means of starvation—wolves with snouts full of porcupine quills, beavers with mouths hopelessly propped open by ingrown incisors, Canada geese wandering futilely across marshes locked in ice.

Moreover, gulls are among the more expendable of Monomoy's birds, a menace to the dwindling tern colonies. Their numbers here are unnaturally large—some fifty thousand pairs—nurtured by the prevalence of open garbage dumps on the nearby mainland. Their scavenging nature leaves them open to fates like the one I had just prevented. Often I have seen them on public beaches and at town landfills with necks or legs encumbered by plastic beer rings. Would I have been so quick to come to this gull's aid if I had found it ensnared so on the mainland? Perhaps I would have done Monomoy's beleaguered terns a favor by leaving the bird to its fate? But there is nothing like the proximity of pain to bend our stiffest ecological prejudices.

Besides, something in the mangled nature of the bird's predicament made it seem especially wrong for such a thing to happen here. The grotesque angularity of its posture had been painful and unseemly. I have seen too many natural contours and shapes—tidal creeks and marshes, gentle pine-studded hills, pond bluffs, rolling heaths, all flowing things on the Cape's mainland—mangled and wrenched by human greed, blindness, and indifference. My sudden, intense passion to help the hobbled gull had sprung in part from the chronic helplessness I usually feel to correct such deformity, to restore the proportion of grace and shape and line, to put things aright again.

It was time to be getting back to the canoe. The tide, and with it the shorebirds, would soon be coming to the marshes at the north end. I struck off east across Monomoy's thin shank toward the ocean beach, crossing several old vehicle tracks shown on my map. These had nearly disappeared, and I had to look closely to see where a slight difference in the vegetation still marked their former passage.

On the beach the surf broke gently and evenly along the shore, where sanderlings ran nonchalantly at the edge of the waves. I stripped again, placed the clothes in my pack, and for nearly a mile walked the August solitude of Monomoy's sands unencumbered, while only the gulls looked on.

IV

It was nearly four o'clock when I reached the canoe again. The tide was coming in rapidly now. I would have to travel fast to reach the marshes before the shorebirds. I dressed and portaged the canoe across the narrow isthmus to the Sound side. Paddling hard up the west shore, I skirted the marshes around Shooter's Island—an island in name only now, but which during the late 1800s was the site of the famous Monomoy Brant Club, a collection of shanties where gentlemen sportsmen from New York congregated for the spring shooting of Monomoy's once-abundant brant flocks. Here I flushed several more snowy egrets, a few willets with their bold black-and-white wing patterns, and some small flocks of Hudsonian godwits, one of Monomoy's "specialties."

Then, toward the north end of the island, I began to see them: an armada of dark silhouettes, still more than a hundred yards out, working their way in with the snaking of the tide. A canoe will work pretty well as a blind if you sit low and quietly in it. I found a tidal creek and worked my way into the edge of the marsh, pulled the canoe up onto a peat bank, and sat down in the bottom to watch.

First to come in were the small, short-legged peep—least and semipalmated sandpipers, sanderlings, ring-necked plovers, the chunkier knots and ruddy turnstones—running and probing just ahead of the tide. Behind them were the larger, long-legged wading birds: short-billed dowitchers, flocks of a hundred or more godwits, tall whimbrels with striped heads and graceful down-curved bills, and neat sets of greater and lesser yellowlegs wading in as if for comparison.

They continued to weave in closer with the advancing shallows, probing in the mud and the shallows with an energetic stitching motion, embroidering the hem of the tide with their own lovely barred-and-streaked patterns of beige, buff, cinnamon, and light gray. No doubt in all their numbers were some of the serious birder's "catches" —a golden plover, a marbled godwit, perhaps even a ruff or a wandering tattler—but I was a novice, content to feast on spectacle, where dimension matched the primal nature of their movement.

Now they approached very close, coming within a few yards of the canoe before parting and flowing around me up into the marsh. As they came near, their separate personalities became more clearly defined. The dow-itchers, greatest in number, with their long, slightly hooked bills and white triangular rump patches, seemed curiously single-minded, probing deeply and rhythmic-ally into the mud, using sensitive, prehensile bill tips to extract small crustaceans and interstitial organisms from the sand grains.

The Hudsonian godwits, by contrast, were taller, with slightly upcurved bills and striking black-and-white tail patterns. They appeared more wary and dignified than the dowitchers, did not probe in so far with their bills, and frequently lifted their graceful heads to look about. Gideon would have chosen godwits for his army.

As the shorebirds advanced and parted around me, I could see, farther out, terns swinging and gliding over the water and, far beyond them, some small dark birds flitting out over the waves, petrels perhaps. From the cord grass behind me came the high, bright chips of sharp-tailed sparrows as they flushed, fluttered up weakly, and dropped back down again. And far inland, across the broad rippling expanse of marsh grass, I heard the muted cacophony of the vast gull colony, one hundred thousand strong. Occasionally, large rafts of shorebirds lifted in a rush of wings and silvery crying, making dark clouds against the lighter real ones gathering from the south. I sat, it seemed, in an element of birds, surrounded as though by rain, wind, and fog, a living fullness that tantalized the mind with visions of an abundance that once rendered waste and decimation so innocent to the minds of men. They formed an electric band of life, so intense, so intent on their probing, running, stalking, dipping, diving, and flitting that I was only minimally regarded, as a wreck or some rock might have been.

The shorebirds passed, the waters encircled the canoe and lifted it off the bottom, and I began to drift with the breeze, turning lightly like a leaf, out into the Sound. The terns now filled the air with their harsh cries, dipping and skimming over the shallows. Most of these were black-billed juveniles that seemed to be drinking and practice-diving rather than fishing in earnest. With the terns I spotted three or four larger birds, striking in appearance: black on top, white underneath, with long red tapered bills tipped with black. These were black skimmers, larger relatives of the terns that can usually be seen in small groups on Monomoy in summer and early fall. Skimmers were nesting on the Cape when Champlain sailed into Nauset Harbor in 1605, but were rapidly extirpated along the New England coast in colonial times by egg hunters. During the past twenty years, after an absence of over two centuries, they have begun nesting on Monomoy again.

A skimmer's bill is an improbable structure at first

glance; its lower mandible is fully one-half again as long as its upper. The skimmer feeds by flying low over the water with its lower bill plowing the surface. When it strikes a small fish, the upper part clamps down. Often the skimmer will work the same "row" of water several times, back and forth, attracting the fish to the surface with its first passage and gathering them up on the next.

In flight the skimmers are handsome, dark-winged birds with flat, slightly arched wingbeats adapted to their unique fishing method. I watched them sail close above the shallows, bright-billed heads dipped low, wings raised high and arched, uttering low *aawrks*. They looked like flying wheelbarrows, or plows, furrowing the contours of the bottom, lowering the bill deep in a channel and raising it to avoid bars. Feeding with the adult skimmers was one immature bird, speckled brown and white above, with a bill still pale in color. It apparently had not yet mastered the skills of its elders, for several times it appeared to misjudge the depth of the water and strike bottom, tripping on its bill, so to speak.

How many uses a single tide could be put to! How many times the same ground could be gone over, harvested and gleaned by a seemingly endless array of bills and beaks, and still yield up fresh sustenance. It seemed a stately procession, a dance of new prey rising up to meet new predators, all riding together on the major rhythms of the tide.

I wanted to stay and see them all go out again, but dusk was coming on and the tide would be against me going back. I took up my paddle and headed back toward the mainland. Since I was already on the west side of the island, I decided to take the cut-through at Harding's

Light into Chatham's Stage Harbor. By the time I reached the entrance to the harbor, the color was draining from the sky in the west and the breeze had freshened from the north. I bucked both wind and tide through the channel, making snail progress, my limbs aching with exhaustion.

It was nearly nine o'clock when I finally entered the inner harbor. In the blackness I could make out the shapes of over a hundred moored boats, from small dinghies to large, expensive yachts. I weaved among their silent, rocking forms, feeling alien and unallied to these vessels and their inhabitants. The smell of steaks barbecuing assailed my nostrils, and I was suddenly ravenous. I saw a charcoal grill standing on the stern deck of one of the larger yachts. Inside its cabin the sounds of talk, laughter, and ice-filled glasses filtered out through lighted windows. I could have scaled the ladder that hung down the stern and made off with the steak without compunction. I felt *outside* this human order and its restraints—an unexpected legacy of my day on Monomoy.

But I paddled on through the harbor, leaving the steaks unmolested, back to the dike where my van was parked. As I rounded the mainland shore, the unaccustomed sound of whippoorwills exploded from its full, dark hills.

An Advent of Scallops

THE SCALLOP SEASON in our town opened on October 6. There was not a great deal of hoopla about it, despite the fact that the previous year had seen one of the most massive sets of seed scallops ever in Cape Cod Bay. The small ridged mollusks lay scattered everywhere on the tidal flats like corrugated quarters, so thick that you could not help crunching their thin shells beneath your boots as you walked about.

I used to get elated at such sights, believing I had only to be patient until the following October to reap a rich harvest of sweet adult bay scallops. But I have since learned by disappointment that seed scallops on the flats are not so much coins as postdated checks on an account whose assets are liable to be frozen before they become negotiable.

The seed *may* occasionally mature into a bumper crop, as it did in the memorable scallop year of 1975. That fall the highways leading to the Cape were filled with young hitchhikers thumbing down from Boston and Providence, many of them cutting college classes for several weeks, to work as shuckers for the commercial fishermen at princely wages. Local forges were backlogged for months with orders for new scallop dredges. The local taverns assumed a boomtown atmosphere, with talk flowing as freely as the liquor and money about new rigs, new boats, new fleets, new lives. But next fall the boom was over, the shuckers were back in school or on welfare, the money had dried up, and only the talk and liquor continued to flow. Commercial scallopers, like the mobile shellfish they pursue, seem to move along in a series of short-lived elations.

The more common fate for the seed, however, at least on the flats, is to be virtually wiped out over the winter. This is because young scallops, unlike the sedentary clams and quahogs, do not bury themselves securely in the sand, but attach themselves to blades of eelgrass by secreting thin filamentous threads called byssus. Unless they are in fairly deep water, these immature scallops are likely to be crushed by heavy winter ice in the bay, or ripped from their fragile moorings by fierce northerly storms which either bury them or carry them in to the exposed flats, where, at low tide, they freeze or fall victim to the omnivorous and insatiable gulls. The scallop pays for its mobility.

Thus, to vary the fiscal metaphor, a set of seed scallops is a kind of promissory note with no collateral. Yet occasionally the law relents and permits confiscation in lieu of payment, and then the part-time amateur scalloper may receive a literal windfall.

It happened that way this year. There was another good set of seed on the flats during the fall, and in December a series of hard northerly blows hit the bay in quick succession. The weekend before Christmas our shellfish warden, Win DuBois, determined that most of the seed crop had been blown in so far that it would almost certainly freeze with the first ice. He obtained permission from the state to open the flats for the taking of the doomed seed, and thereby precipitated, by default, a scallop rush of a scope not seen since that legendary 1975 season.

This rush, involving only the small, uneconomical seed scallops, created a mostly local and noncommercial stir. Still, when I drove down to Ellis Landing late in the morning three days after the official announcement, cars and trucks were backed up along the road a quarter-mile from the beach. A milling crowd, carrying rakes, waders, and buckets, filled the parking lot, moving out toward the beach. There was a holiday or circus feeling in the air, and I could see Win DuBois, tall and lean, moving slowly about in the center of it all like a ringmaster.

From the beach was an impressive sight: over six hundred people spread out across the wide flats, dressed in colorful winter wool and nylon garments—bright oranges, reds, greens, and blues. It was a fine winter day, crisp, clear, a few degrees above freezing, the whole scene intensely lit by the low winter sun. There was a constant come and go of figures across the exposed half-mile expanse of flats, with a line of steady, industrious raking going on just beyond the water's edge.

During that first week no permits were required or quotas imposed, and in our unregulated greed we were all, in a way, a fine example of adaptation and specialization, though after the same quarry. Just as different tern species feed on the same species of sand eel at different depths, so we worked the scallops in different zones: women in London Fogs and fur-trimmed boots gleaned the leftovers on the beach and the damp inner flats, kids in sneakers worked the shallows, while grownups in hip boots and waders raked the deeper waters.

I walked out as far as the first ice-gouged potholes, into which the scallops had been washed in large mounds, and began raking. Now and then we were warned by Win's bullhorn from the shore: *"Not over your knees!"*—not as a safety precaution for us but as protection for the seed in deeper waters which still had a chance of surviving.

As always, this scallop boom spawned an ingenious variety of rigs, buckets, and homemade contrivances for harvesting the shellfish. In addition to the standard scallop rakes, there were quahog rakes, clam rakes, pitchforks, garden rakes jury-rigged with wire baskets, shovels, and even a few cranberry scoops. They were raked in blindly or picked at carefully. The water was lightly choppy, obscuring the bottom, so that the bunched mounds were usually found by feel or chance. One man had rigged a floating wooden box with a glass bottom and pushed it ahead of him, peering through it and picking only the biggest scallops off the bottom, then plopping them in the box—until at last his own harvest obscured his view.

There was no sense of competition among the rakers and pickers amid such plenty, only differing strategies as to how to get the most scallops ashore in the least time with the least effort. A full bushel of scallops weighs about a hundred pounds. It took less than ten minutes to harvest a bushel in the deeper holes, but it then had to be carried half a mile to the landing to be unloaded— a process referred to as the "scallops' revenge."

To accomplish this, the harvested scallops were loaded and hauled ashore in an equally imaginative array of vehicles. These ranged from the standard net scallop bags or burlap bags, slung over the shoulder, to Glad Bags, plastic buckets, garbage cans, pans, sleds, shopping carts, baby carriages, contractors' wheelbarrows, and imaginative amphibious devices such as clam baskets set in large inner tubes that were roped to a wheeled frame so that the rig floated in deep water and rolled on the flats. One man even brought his motorcycle out on the flats with a milk carton tied on the back.

My own rig, I think, was as good as any. Devised by my father, it consisted of a plastic milk case mounted on an axle with two baby carriage wheels and fitted with various metal flanges attached to the rim into which the tongs of my rake fit snugly, thus forming a firm but easily removable handle with which to draw it in and out over the flats.

Despite the lack of individual competition, the prospect of such a perishable abundance bred haste and greed, producing a procession of Dantesque tableaux across that wide plain. Normally sedentary residents struggled under unwieldy burdens on the verge of cardiac arrest. One man appeared monstrously pregnant, wrestling with an enormous burlap sackful as large as his own torso. He tripped at one point over a rock he could not see and dropped the sack forward onto the hard mud, audibly smashing most of the brittle scallops inside.

At one point I worked near a three-man team. Two of them stood nearby holding plastic sacks, waiting for the third to arrive with their rakes. As they watched me piling rakeful after rakeful of scallops into my basket, I could sense them growing increasingly restive and frustrated. Finally, no longer able to stand patiently by as I raked it in, they rolled up their sleeves and thrust their bare arms down into the icy water, furtively at first, but then with unabashed, gullish greed.

For once, in fact, our own greed visibly displaced that of the gulls. By the thousands the birds stood or swarmed in the shallows at either end of the long human crowd, giving raucous voice to the food frenzy we were all too intensely busy with to express ourselves. It was an appetite justified by the moribund feast, however, as we reaped the scallops' misfortune.

At the peak of the harvest there were some one thousand people out on the flats, numbers far exceeding any town meeting turnout. There were, I suspect, more local residents gathered together that day for a common purpose than at any time in the town's history.

Before the sun went down we raked and appropriated some fifteen hundred bushels of seed scallops, with full state approval, laboring under no tax caps or budget limits, with no limits at all, for that matter, no competing interest groups, no fights between conservation and development, no hurt feelings, litigations, or questions of historic appropriateness.

For once, instead of futilely worrying about how to preserve the character of our town, we were sustaining it by living it. For once I could agree with those public officials who facilely assure us that we all want the same things. *Yes, yes,* came our tacit cry as we rolled, dragged, lugged, and carted our booty ashore, puffing like steam engines in the cold air. *Here, here,* the gulls proclaimed, echoing our assent and affirmation: this sustains us, this feeds us abundance in the depth of the year, brings us life out of death, and draws us willingly, passionately, into the traces of the sea's rhythms.

The sun wheeled and danced on our heads, sending

out reflected rays from our wavering shadows on the bright winter waters. The wide sweeping arm of the Cape curved around us to the east and swung north, like a sickle.

Star People

ONE OF THE great pleasures of late spring and early summer is to sleep outside on our deck under the stars. Before the summer haze has veiled the sky and summer insects send us scurrying indoors again, it is a seasonal delight simply to lie, in relative comfort, open to the unenclosed night. One never knows what one will see.

Some years we can do this as early as late April, when the peeper chorus in the bog is still strong and the herring run is at its peak. Then the effervescence of frog pipings below us seems to match, or express, the inundation of stars overhead, and from a mile away the screams and guttural coughs of night-feeding gulls at the run carry clearly through the unleaved trees.

On early May nights we can sometimes observe the Aquarid meteor shower, an admittedly modest display compared with the Perseids of August or the Leonids of November, but still enough so that every hour several streaks of pale-orange light go stabbing, like sudden needles, across the eastern sky above rising Pegasus. And so we go to sleep among stars and peepers and the cries of herring gulls, and wake to early light and birds—cardinals, chickadees, titmice, and crows—the resonant tolling of the East Dennis church, and nylon sleeping bags heavily sprinkled with beaded, sparkling dew.

I have noticed that the first night or two outside is often a restless one. Perhaps the mind, after a winter's sleep indoors, is simply uneasy in such unwonted, unconfined space. Part of it, though, is simply getting accustomed to the noises. The night, even our relatively domesticated night, is full of sounds that normally go unheard indoors, even with the windows open. As my eyes begin to unfocus and the stars dissolve, the dark ground below the deck is full of rustlings and scratchings in last year's leaves, reminding me again that most mammals are nocturnal. Even when the great nighttime noisemakers—the peepers, whippoorwills, and owls—are silent, the air is full of liquid drippings from the trees and clawed scuttlings along the roof; a bird warbles briefly in its sleep from its midnight perch; in the pre-dawn gloom the leathery whispers of bats after lingering moths brush my ears, and the strident bark of a seal from Sealand a half-mile away carries with a timbre designed to pierce the crash of waves. I wake, somewhere at sea, and am glad for the familiar songs of dawn birds to help tell me where I am.

If the night is not silent, the sky, of course, is no longer pristine. Occasional jets, blinking red and green, sail smoothly overhead, coming or going from Europe, carrying sleeping bodies, couched and padded in pressurized hulls. Miles below, my eyes track them. On moonlit nights their vapor trails stretch out in silver plumes, a sight which, in visual splendor, rivals that of the old clipper ships. I wonder about them, those night passengers so unaware of me, and what motivations have propelled them on such fantastic voyages across my nighttime sky, voyages at once trivial and heroic.

Frequently a bright white star near the horizon will begin to rise, slowly but noticeably, up toward the zenith, like a tiny bubble in a bottle of concentrated shampoo: a satellite, reminding me that the Space Age, though put on hold from time to time, has irrevocably begun.

Last month—and for the only time in my life—I thought I had actually spotted a UFO. In the eastern sky a pulsing arc of colored lights, like the rim of the spaceship in *Close Encounters*, seemed to hover for several minutes and then slowly began to approach. When it finally came close enough, I saw that the lights were flashing not some tonally coded extraterrestrial message, but "HAPPY BIRTHDAY SUMNER!"

Terrestrial lights impinge on the sky as well. From our deck the western horizon burns nightly with the pink-orange glow of sodium vapor lights from a small shopping center several miles away. Much nearer, less than a hundred yards to the north, the incandescent streetlight on the corner casts its soft and companionable pool of light down onto the road. Now and then pairs of headlights, like parallel comets in reverse, hurl their spreading tails ahead of them over the black pavement.

Despite these and other artificial lights, our night sky remains blessedly uncluttered. On clear, moonless nights, when my eyes have become fully adjusted to the dark, I become aware of the soft, curved, tilted band of the Milky Way. How rarely we see it, or even look for it anymore. Yet this immense and subtle spectacle was a nightly visual experience and a deep mythic presence to our earliest civilizations. Whatever the Milky Way meant to the ancients, however, modern astronomy steps in and hands me its glasses. I look through them, edgewise, into the thickening center of our galaxy—a whirling disk of star clusters, cloud nebulas, and cosmic dust 100,000 light years across—and feel myself swung to sleep in the crook of its immense spiral arms.

The stars still beckon and challenge us in their alien distance. Unlike the moon and the planets, they remain as they were to primitive man, unattainable and inaccessible except in imagination. It is true we have launched rockets at them, placing aboard tokens of our civilization in the infinitesimal hope that somewhere, sometime, they may be intercepted, if not until our own sun has gone dark. We also now shout continuous silent messages at them through our radio telescope transmitters, yet they keep their counsel. What is it we ask of them, or they of us?

A partial answer came to me one moonless night a week or so ago. I lay on my back on the deck, stretched out under a light blanket, looking up at the sky. It was a remarkably still night, cool but humid, so that the stars, while clear and plentiful, were not overwhelming in abundance. They lacked that hard, glittering brilliance they have in winter. They seemed closer, more human somehow, so that I felt I might climb up one of the oaks beside the deck and gather them like fruit.

Now and then a long, thin, orange-tinged meteor would cruise briefly across the zenith and disappear into the folded silence. There was no moon, no sound of surf or traffic. Only the stars held sway, hanging down out of the vaulted night like the hieroglyphs of old, edited for me now out of the chaos of their original plenitude by the fine filtering screen of a slight night haze, which made the major constellations stand out in compelling clarity.

While I have always been sensitive to the splendor of the stars, constellations, even in childhood, have never held much interest for me. I considered them weak astronomical fictions, arbitrary groupings, flat distortions of the reality of interstellar depths. They always seemed to me evidence, not of the richness but of the desperation of the ancient imagination. How arbitrary and unconvincing they seemed—poor, partial figures, overlapping and cluttered. Even their official boundaries remained undefined until an international committee established them by fiat in 1930. I was unimpressed. Except for the Big Dipper, what sky pattern is really self-evident?

And so, with youthful disdain, I dismissed them as a childish game, a pointless exercise for Boy Scouts, at best an outmoded aid to navigators or amateur stargazers in locating individual stars. As a result, I know very few constellations today, or their stars. There is the Pole Star, of course, at the end of the Little Dipper; bright Sirius, too, though I never remember what part of the Large Dog it is supposed to form; Aldebaran, though I cannot see the great Bull whose red, glowing eye it is supposed to be; and a few others.

But on that calm night, with the constellations in screened relief, I suddenly felt what they must have been to the ancients: a great and enduring comfort. They looked up and saw, or thought they saw, eternal patterns and idealized types of humanity. They saw familiar objects—scales, tables, arrows, harps, nets—and the shapes of domestic and wild animals, all punched permanently into the sky, revolving and ticking away in their fixed courses forever. The mantle of the universe, in other words, bore a human pattern to their eyes, though it took an act of imagination to see it and to hold them there.

Modern man has largely abandoned the art of stargazing for the science of astronomy. We no longer believe in the mythic or astrologic significance of the constellations, and there are better entertainments indoors. Their existence required our active participation and faith, which may be incompatible with the modern temperament. I think now this may have been at the root of my youthful disdain: I wanted definite statements, cool, unambiguous responses from the stars, and that is not what they offered. So I shunned them and went inside to watch TV.

Yet we still have that need to see human shapes in the sky. Our little specks of flashing metal and blinking birthday messages will not do. The growing obliteration of the night sky in our cities and along our highways with the sprawl of high-intensity vapor lamps (which has rendered several large observatories practically useless in many parts of the country) may seem to remove the question, as putting a roof over our head gives us the illusion of controlling the weather. But the great unanswered questions of the stars remain, and in places like this, where the sky is still clear, they can yet be heard.

They are still there for us to see: Ursa, Perseus, the clustered Pleiades, sturdy Orion after his long winter's chase, plunging downward through the burning night. Our fathers and our forefathers have told us so, and looking up, we know they did not conjure them out of nothing or for nothing. They are still there, those old human shapes. Yet on nights like this, when they hang down in such tantalizing and yet unrecognized outline, when our partial and unpracticed knowledge of the sky fails us and we feel, in our closeted lives, far removed from any living connection with the universe, the ancient syntax of the stars begins to go, the mythical forms dissolve and swim, unformed, through the night, and we are left again with naked eyes, staring up at a cold, unpeopled sky.

A Summer Place

L AST WEEKEND (it seems ages ago now) I attended, for the third year going, an old-fashioned Labor Day family clambake on the beach. As one of a handful of invited "friends of the family" at this affair, I enjoy a somewhat privileged position that gives me participation rights in its pleasures without the social responsibilities that go with any family reunion. I am no one's uncle or cousin, and everyone, even the children, calls me by my first name.

The clambake is the climax of an annual week-long series of dinners, sing-alongs, softball games, and other events involving over forty people from several states ranging from great-grandtoddlers to the family matriarch, an octogenarian who serves as official piano player for the gathering and still takes her turn at bat in the ball games. Although this reunion is only a dozen years old, it has already taken on some aspects of a ritual. The same people come, the same events take place, year after year. Nothing unusual is planned or happens beyond a rare rainout or an occasional trip to the local emergency room when one of the more adventurous grandchildren breaks a collarbone or tears a knee ligament.

All family reunions are essentially alike, and this clambake is like a hundred others which occur along Cape Cod's shores every year as they have for more than a hundred years with little change. As such it takes its place among a scattered and cyclical myriad of such local family gatherings over the years, a human activity that, in such perspective, begins to assume the dimension of the tide itself.

This particular gathering is more fortunate than most in its setting, for the participants have over a thousand feet of private beach on Cape Cod Bay all to themselves. Some of the family are friends with the owners of one of the Cape's dwindling number of sea camps, who loan the beach out to them for the weekend. (By Labor Day the camp has been closed for nearly two weeks.) The beach not only provides spacious isolation, but the flats offshore are strewn with small boulders covered with rockweed. The day before the clambake the men dig a six-foot-square pit on the upper beach and then go out and gather rocks and seaweed that will heat and steam the clams, lobsters, and corn the following afternoon.

The beach itself, like the clambake, does not change appreciably from one Labor Day to the next, though even after a few years small variations are apparent in both. People age (never one's contemporaries, it seems, only those on either side). The weather changes. The beach retreats a little. The pit is dug roughly in the same place each time, but this year was the first that evidence of the previous year's bake was uncovered. The rocks, however, were cracked with the heat and could not be used again.

The clambake this year was held just before high tide,

a near moon tide at that, with a northwest wind blowing, so that there was some half-serious joking as to whether the lobsters would be boiled rather than steamed. The bay, rough and dark, full of weeds and animals of late summer churned up by several days of onshore wind, lapped at table legs and volleyball net poles.

Only a few years ago, in the face of such threatening seas, the small children would have watched from the security of their mothers' laps or been content to play on the upper beach. But the boys, a half-dozen or so of them, now perched on the verge of adolescence, ran out and challenged the waves, breasting the choppy swells and flinging handfuls of floating dead man's fingers at one another, while jellyfish stung their bare chests and feet. When they emerged from the water, lean and dripping, they gathered close together halfway up the dune face, the way gull flocks do on the outer beach, gnawing lobsters and sucking clams.

All of the adults are very conscientious and careful with the beach they have borrowed. All litter is meticulously picked up, and after the bake the pit is completely filled in and smoothed over. At the end of the afternoon I am always struck with how so many people can use so small a stretch of beach so intensely and leave so little evidence of their having been there.

At one point in this year's outing two small girls were flinging themselves in helicopter twirls off a dune crest. One of the aunts quickly scolded them off, telling them sharply, "You're not supposed to do that." I felt a bit guilty, since I had been watching them with pleasure and had not said anything. It was, I knew, the proper environmental response to make. But I also felt that twinge, that surge of resentment, when either I or someone else must curb a child's instinctive pleasure in playing with a landscape. It is unfortunate, not only to break the salutary contact, the physical intimacy of child and beach, but to teach him or her that jumping off a dune, an activity no one thought twice about engaging in a generation ago, is now somehow wrong in itself, an act inherently destructive or immoral, rather than behavior no longer allowable as a result of excessive human numbers.

Halfway through the afternoon of the clambake, while most of the adults relaxed with their third beer and the children raced up and down the tide-narrowed beach, I went for a walk up the dirt road to explore the now-closed summer camp. It was a familiar sight, bringing back a flood of memories of college summers when I worked as a counselor at another sailing camp not far from here. After camp closed I was always the last to go, reluctant to leave this privileged summer playground of Cape Cod, not knowing then that I would someday return to stay.

Now, nearly another lifetime since, I found myself walking a familiar, abandoned landscape, along the deserted sand roads, past the drained swimming pool, the empty netless tennis courts, the stacks of floats and rows of sailboats, the closed bare-walled cabins and buildings stuffed with mats and canoes, the whole place filled with the ghosts of recently departed campers, alive with this year's memories deepened with overtones of years of anonymous repetition, like the family clambake I had left on the beach.

Once I naively believed that such places would always be what they were simply because they should be. I had never considered then such things as property values, tax rates, investment potential, and development pressures. Now it was impossible to walk casually through such a place without thinking, How long? How long before this one goes the way of other local camps that have vanished? Sea camps in particular are endangered species here, diminishing in the face of skyrocketing values and taxes on waterfront property and the traditionally low level of use, or "minimal capital return" on such properties.

Eventually, in most cases, towns cannot afford to buy these lands and owners cannot afford not to sell. Many similar bayfront properties in our town have been turned into so-called "exclusive planned living communities" in recent years, and two other camps just down the beach are currently up for sale. Even as I walked I seemed to see yet another posh condominium project unrolling like a mylar overlay across this casual landscape, put there by yet another community-minded corporate developer with environmentally respectful bulldozers.

Whenever I find myself drifting into this kind of cynical anticipation, I force myself to stop and ask why. We can no longer afford to be self-righteously vague about our emotional environmental prejudices. Too much is at stake. We must examine them to see if they are false or sentimental and, if not, precisely where their truth lies. If we oppose some particular fate for a landscape, we must be able to say why. If we are going to be unreasonable in our demands, let us be sure to have good reasons for being so.

What, for instance, would be lost, damaged, or irreversibly diminished by having this camp, or any like it, turned into, say, a condominium development? In many ways, such a conversion would not create a much more intense use of the land than now exists. The number of year-round residents living in such a development might, depending on local zoning codes, actually be less than the number of campers here in summer. And no doubt they would be much more environmentally conscientious about the dunes and beaches than the campers, having considerably more vested interest to protect. The camp, with its dozens of buildings, tennis courts, and network of roads, is hardly a "wilderness," or even open space, in the strict sense. True, the present structures are considerably smaller and less pretentious than the town houses and "beachfront clusters" that would probably replace them, so that a certain colorful informality might be lost. Yet they are just about as numerous and occupy nearly as much land area as the buildings in a well-planned development.

It is also possible to argue both ways concerning the effects of modern development here on local taxes, school populations, water and sewer systems, offshore shellfish beds, the "character" of the town, and so on. But in the end these issues tend to become both so detailed and abstract that they miss the heart of the matter.

But what is the heart of the matter? Why does the potential development of a camp like this one fill me with such a strong sense of loss? Is it nothing more than selfish nostalgia, merely the wish to continue to hold Labor Day clambakes and walk the winter beach here undisturbed? If no more than that, is such a position defensible in the face of the potential profit to the owners, the jobs to the builders, the pleasure of hundreds of future residents, and the possible tax benefits to the town itself from such a conversion?

There is something more, though, something that has

to do not with the intensity or density, but with the relative *permanency* of occupation such a change would bring. This particular camp represents one of the few remaining stretches of the old bay landscape here, the gently sloping, pine-studded plain ending in modest sea bluffs or low dunes, rarely sought out or used by the old Cape Codders except as windswept pastureland or for Sunday-afternoon walks on calm days. And before them, one can infer from scattered artifacts found on the property, local Indian tribes hunted sporadically through its woods and came down to its shores in season to gather the clams, quahogs, and scallops that still draw us to the long flats sweeping out from its beach.

In season—that is the clue. For though many camp owners must increasingly seek year-round income from such property by hosting winter conferences or environmental seminars, this camp, like the uses that have preceded it, is still primarily seasonal; and that, to me, forms its greatest value.

It is still seasonal in a way the Cape once was and largely is no more. As seasonal cycles diminish in their importance to us, "The Season" itself grows longer and longer at both ends of the summer until its tendrils threaten to touch around the tree of the year. As the winter population continues to grow and more and more summer cottages are converted to year-round dwellings, our whole attitude toward the land becomes one of more permanent and more possessive occupation.

A summer camp represents not only a limited but a periodic use of the land. Such use unconsciously recognizes the need for a recovery period in our dealings with the land, not so much for such measurable things as water tables or tree growth, but for the land itself and our perception of it. We need to leave a place some time that is not ours, as a farmer leaves a field fallow through several seasons in order to ensure a future crop. It is important, for both its life and ours, that its grass grow uncut, that oak encroach on pine unmanaged, that its rabbit and quail run unseen for long stretches of time.

Despite its roads, its buildings, and all the other paraphernalia of human use, such a place can still function as a kind of seasonal wilderness, when "who knows what" can happen: when the sea might break through the dunes in winter, or a stand of locust trees blow down in an autumn northeaster, or moving sands begin to bury an old boathouse. Even more important, such events would at present pose no great threat or disaster to anyone's investment, and that is both health and wealth to a land and the people who use it. It is a mean life that puts its faith in concrete footings and seawalls rather than in the natural rhythms around it. The individual who cannot afford change in his surroundings cannot afford change in himself.

In the end, such places of seasonal occupation remind us that all human ventures—emotional, economic, or architectural—are essentially transient and cyclical and should not be prolonged beyond their season. Historically, the hallmark of human enterprises on these shores— shipbuilding, farming, weir fishing, woodcutting, summer cottaging and camping—has been, until quite recently, that they have all left the possibility of something replacing them, the potential of a new rendezvous with the land for the next generation. There has always been the sense that something more, something further, can still readily happen here between people and the land—a quality that is at the heart of the attraction of "summer places." But condominiums and shopping malls and most other forms of dense, permanent modern development in these areas erase that possibility. Not only in their size, but in their complete and total disposal of the landscape in terms of direct economic value (where even areas of open space, required for sewage systems or storm water runoff, are sold as "amenities"), they seem like final, monolithic phrases carved irrevocably into the face of the earth. As one local resident put it, they are "the end of the story."

With these long thoughts I finally gained the beach again, a few hundred feet west of the clambake site. I walked back, picking up here and there tennis balls that had been lost in the waves, floated up by the longshore current, and washed ashore again by the tide.

The feast was done. People were already gathering up volleyball poles, horseshoe stakes, folding tables, trash barrels, chairs, blankets, and children—stealing away like the once-patronized Arabs, not to be seen here again for another year. The clam pit had been filled in and two men stood beside it, raking the sand smooth. They were abetted in their efforts by the tide, which continued to creep up on the beach, slipping into, gradually filling, and at last erasing the marks of innumerable heels, hands, elbows, and buttocks.

Another Sunset

T HE WADERS, CHEAP when I bought them five years ago, leak badly now. The haft on the rake is so rusty I expect it to snap off each time I use it. And, as usual, my shellfish license is lost somewhere in a can full of old bus schedules, bird checklists, and tide charts.

But what the hell, it's October, it's four o'clock on a Friday afternoon, the tide is almost out, and the quahog flats have just opened. So I dig out the license, gather up waders, rake, and bucket, and throw them in the back of our '71 bus, give the side door a hip check to close it, and rattle down to the landing at the end of Doone Road.

It's cloudy on the beach, in the low fifties, with a light northeast wind wrinkling the shallows offshore. Win is there, standing next to his silver Subaru, dwarfing it, long and lanky in hip boots and baseball cap, a stereotype of the New England shellfish warden. For this first week he has opened the seedbed, a rocky area close inshore, for scratching. Already a half-dozen people are out there, clawing at the stony mud with clam rakes and

quahog rakes, prying the prized littlenecks out from
between the cobbles.

The seedbed, a narrow strip several hundred feet long,
runs just in front of the old Catholic seminary, now converted into oceanfront condominiums whose slanted roofs
and balconies plow like ship prows toward the beach.
The scratchers seem oblivious to them, however, and the
gulls and the flats look as wild as ever. Win comes over
and tells me he is worried about the small stream issuing
through the dunes next to the new development. Its
mouth has shifted some fifty feet east recently, due to
the removal of an old stone jetty by the developers, he
says. He is afraid that this will shunt the streamwater
away from his seedbed and hurt it. Quahogs like fresh
water? I ask. Oh yes, he replies, they use the food in the
stream. Maybe, but, like the rest of us, he doesn't really
sound certain of what he says.

I work the rock pile with the others for ten minutes or
so, getting a couple of dozen small littlenecks, checking
them with my ring. Clammers here are issued two-inch
steel rings with their licenses; if a clam fits longways
through the ring without touching, it is legally undersize
and must be replaced. Win, however, checks suspiciously
small clams not with a ring but with the first two joints
of his index finger, a fine relic of Anglo-Saxon legality.

Having had enough of this hard labor, I head out over
the flats toward the distant water for chowder quahogs.
My triangulation point is a pair of large, fucus-skirted
boulders about a quarter-mile out. Here the water is
calf-high and still running out against the wind. There
are only four other scratchers in the area, two couples.
I pick a likely-looking patch of eelgrass, set my feet, and
begin drawing the rake tines through sand and grass.

It is always a pleasure to come out here when these

flats first open in October. Part of it is the contrast with summer clamming, which I do rarely. Now, in high autumn, feet are shod against nipping clams, people are fewer, the eelgrass is considerably shorter and sparser, and the water much clearer.

It is good digging immediately. With almost every draw of the tines there is the sudden catch, the squeak, the teasing of the quahog out of the mud; then, with the long wooden handle pointed straight up, I sift out the mud and wormtubes and seaweed and empty scallop shells in the running tide to reveal, at last, the gray-blue, concentric-ribbed hinged and valved mollusk to the light.

Occasionally I drop a clam from the rake and must wait for the water to clear as the current slides the mud and silt away, leaving the nugget exposed on the bottom. I also stop now and then, for no particular reason, just so as not to be drawn too completely into the digging process, not to miss the flats for the clams.

My initial honey patch yields a little more than half a bucket before giving out. I move around for a while, not finding much. Then, a little after five, just as the flood tide begins, one of the other scratchers, a woman in her sixties in hip boots, stalks over to me. She carries a knotted string bag full of quahogs slung over her shoulder. The man with her follows behind, drawing after him an inflated inner tube with a plastic milk carton in it, also full. She says they have gotten more than their quota, and would I like a few? "We just have a lot of fun out here," she says. There is an accent, not old Cape, exactly, but southern New England. He asks me about the seed scallops on the flats, what will happen to them. Wind and ice likely, I answer. She puts a dozen or so large chowders in my bucket, making it nearly full.

Shortly after 5:30 I quit, though I could probably

balance a few more clams above the rim of the bucket. I have been out for nearly an hour. The left leg of my waders is full of water up to my knee, and it is getting hard to see things in the water. With the bucket hooked onto the rake tines and the handle over my shoulder, I trudge back in across the flats to the beach, up the wooden steps that climb the eroding bank, down the backslope of the dune to the car, where I deposit the clams, take off the waders, wring out my left sock, and replace it with the spare one I carry.

Then I walk back up the plank path to the crest of the dune and look out. All but two of the figures out on the flats have come in now. The sky is still a solid cloud cover, but there is a crack around its western edge like a pot lid slightly raised, a crack reddening and intensifying by the moment. I can tell it is going to be another one of those patented, end-of-the-day apocalyptic blazes, so common out on the flats at the end of cloudy days, yet so unexpected unless you recognize all the signs from having been out here before in October. I've seen it before, but I decide to stay and watch.

The wind is still east and raw, however, and a cold dampness begins to sift uncomfortably through the open weave of my sweater. I go back to the car and get the blanket. It is an old purple plaid wool blanket that served as a family picnic and beach blanket thirty years ago on summer trips in my father's Plymouths in New Jersey, that later became the official car blanket in his Pontiacs when we moved to West Virginia, and that I somehow inherited ten years ago when my parents moved to the Cape. I have kept it in my VW bus, using it as a cushion for lumber and firewood and as a ground cover when working under the car. It is more than a little torn now, and full of oil stains, but still warm and durable and just right as I wrap myself up in it and sit on the wooden railing at the top of the dune to watch what I know will happen, what I have seen happen so many times before, and have even described in print.

This, I realize, is why I decided to stay: precisely because I have seen it all before. It is a luxury to indulge in, to watch something so well known, so well remembered, that one is free of the responsibility to record, or even to see well. I am content just to sit here, wrapped in the mantle of this old blanket, with a full bucket of clams in the car behind me (I'll stop at my parents' house on the way home and drop off a dozen or so of the littlenecks), just to sit and gather whatever may come to me, expecting nothing but the familiar, like a child listening to a favorite bedtime story.

A field of light, wind, and sand sprawls before me, a darkening and varied plain full of the cries and laughter of gulls—*chuka-chuka-chuka*—and the single dark figure of a man walking in toward shore from east to west across patches of wrinkled water, curved rises of sand, his boots making slip-slap progress through the shallow puddles. He moves like an astronaut, with forced dignity, across a wet moonscape. How odd it is that filmmakers have not yet exploited this remarkable landscape or, if they have, have not invented an action, a proper narrative to fit it. It should be one of gentle starkness and exposure, of some endlessly proferred and withdrawn mystery, of careless fecundity and small, hidden burrowed things startled into life by the sharp prod of steel points.

Now the intensification and anticipation of color at the horizon has reached its peak. The red sun appears as I knew it would at the top edge of the cloud-crack. Its light locks my eyes, sucks air from my chest, and I am thinking, God oh God are we ever prepared for this? It is like nothing I have ever seen before. It descends softly, out of the soft gray cloud cover, like an egg, like a turd, like a huge red placenta. It seems to bend as it descends, like a vinegared egg going through a bottleneck, so that I am sure it will bounce when it hits the horizon.

A yellowlegs flies in and begins to feed at the edges of a large tide pool on the beach just below me. It probes for a while with its long bill, bobbing and moving its head with that jerky yet smooth motion of Indonesian dancers, then flies several yards to the east and feeds again. Each time it flies it announces itself with loud continuous cries—*!che!che!che!*—like an emergency ambulance screaming its presence along an empty highway: *I am he! I am he! I am he!* Each time it flies and cries, I look away from the sun and find its long, graceful sculptured body in flight, moving in a round green afterimage on my retina, as in a spotlight, or a gunsight.

Far to the east, across the bay, unseen windows on unseen houses on the bluffs of Eastham suddenly catch the sun's rays and send them back to my eyes. They seem like the bright, brief blazes of signal fires set on the dark hills at night by the vanished Nausets, not so much to keep themselves warm as to keep the sun alive until morning.

Now the deep red ball of the sun has emerged in full. There is just enough room for its complete bulk in the space between cloud cover and horizon, so that it looks as if it were being squeezed in a press and might suddenly burst, like some nuclear appendix, spurting and shooting its fiery poison through all the folds and creases of the sky.

It does not burst, though. It does not even (as it usually does) suddenly blaze up to flood the flats and illuminate the underbelly of the cloud cover with irradiant, transmuting light. Instead, this time, it only casts a thin, fading reddish light over near things, over the weathered wooden railing on which I sit, over the yellowing dune grass, igniting it, over the white eroding sand of the bluff itself, as the wet wind blows steadily across my cheek and the freckled, leprous beachplum leaves flap behind me with a sound like wounded birds.

It goes on with a steady, measured, uninterrupted progress, the sunball sinking, contracting to a dome, an arc, a curved paring, a vanishing point. And at the very moment of extinguishment (though it may only be some spasm of my tired eye muscles) the hanging line of ragged clouds above the horizon shudders, actually *moves* up and down, once, twice, as though the plane of light in which the clouds exist has suddenly shifted beneath the curve of the earth. And then it is over.

Ice Age Art

SOMETIMES, FOR ALL its geologic youth, the
Cape seems tediously old and barren. This morning, for instance, a glacial wind is strafing the land with
gale force, shattering and flattening the surf on the Bay,
whipping the beach grass into waves of blond fire,
hurling dune sand into the tidal creeks of Quivett Marsh,
and rushing up the low, morainal hills in which our house
is set. The bright sunlight is harsh, violent, alien, careen-
ing around the yard off rocks, walls, frozen slopes. The
birds all huddle somewhere out of sight in coniferous
cover, and the bare gray oaks rise like stone sculpture
from the hard ground, rocking stiffly and casting lean,
crooked shadows across the pale lawn.

Though such elemental energy usually stirs me, I am
not sure I am ready yet for another winter, ready to
withdraw, into this house, into myself, to keep life alive
through stored-up wood, stored-up memories, waiting
for the renewal of spring. I find myself recalling an
exhibit of "Ice Age Art" that I saw a few years ago at the
American Museum of Natural History in New York City.

At the time it compelled me with a force I could not account for, but now I think I begin to understand.

The exhibit brought together a wide collection of Paleolithic artifacts, dating from 30,000 B.C. to 10,000 B.C. It included wall paintings, relief sculptures, decorative jewelry, carved stone "Venus" fertility figures, engravings done on mammoth tusks, bear bones, and reindeer antlers, and, by way of eclectic variety, the mummified foot of a baby mammoth, complete with reddish hair. The art objects came mostly from the cave-rich region of southwestern Europe, but also from Germany, Italy, and the Near East. By necessity, many of the displays were copies, casts, or photographic reproductions of the originals, and there were also large photo murals of the caves' interiors and environs.

Cave art, the most ancient manifestation we have of the human imagination, was discovered less than a century ago. The most famous examples of all, the magnificent animal murals in the caves at Lascaux, in the Dordogne region of southern France, were not found until 1940, just after the fall of France to the Nazis. I had seen prints of the Lascaux frescoes many times before, but surrounded by life-size color reproductions, I was struck anew at the vividness and vitality of the figures, how precisely the artists had managed to capture the essential character of each animal—a giant bison in its final death agony, leaping wild boars, a herd of reddish reindeer moving across what was then frozen tundra, magnificent Picasso-like bulls, and pregnant horses with warm, shaggy coats.

Using pulverized ocher for pigment, flat bones for palettes, reeds for brushes, and animal-fat lamps for light, these Stone Age artists had utilized their primitive materials to optimum advantage. Art historians are now in general agreement as to the high order of art represented by these paintings, citing such sophisticated techniques as the careful use of shading and the employment of the natural contours of the limestone walls and ceilings to accentuate the muscular structure of the animals.

Less agreement exists on other matters, however. How did art of such a high quality flourish in such primitive and harsh conditions, and what was its function? These cave artists worked during the end of the last glacial period, some fifteen thousand years ago, at the edge of retreating walls of ice, huddled in rock shelters against an arctic climate. Although this may appear an unlikely place for art to flourish, they were also witness to great processions of a marvelous variety of wildlife, which they hunted at close quarters and which must have stirred their imaginations deeply.

Still these works are remarkable, not only in their quality but in their very existence. Obviously they must have possessed some great importance for the artists and for their tribes. Often located in the deepest and most inaccessible portions of the caves, as far as a half-mile from the entrance, they required enormous effort and endurance to complete. A female skeleton, found deep inside one of the caves, was laced from head to foot in strings of carved red beads estimated to have required over one thousand hours of labor. Who in a Stone Age culture had a thousand hours to spare, and for what purpose? A large photo showed an elaborate wall painting and, on the ground below it, the footprints of the artist leading away from his finished work; apparently neither he nor anyone else ever returned to it. Another photograph, taken near the entrance of one of the caves, showed a small, winding, underground river; running beside it, on the sandy banks, were the intermingled tracks of three Paleolithic children, 150 centuries old. I realized with a start that, if any of those children survived, there was a good chance I was looking at the footprints of one of my direct ancestors.

Most discussion about the "intent" of this artwork centers around phrases like "hunting magic" and "fertility rites," and what we know about later primitive cultures seems to support such interpretations. But there is really too little to go on for definitive answers, and what little we do know seems subject to revision. One common line motif, usually juxtaposed with drawings of horses or cattle, has traditionally been interpreted as a "spear," thus supporting the theory of "hunting magic." More recent examinations, however, suggest that these lines actually represent spears of wheat, and that their juxtaposition with herbivores, often pregnant ones, was intended as a symbol of spring, or perpetual renewal, when the deer again flowed like brown rivers through the barren passes of the Pyrenees and wild grain and berries began to reappear.

Such strict separation of these art works into "religious," "historical," "commemorative," and other functions is probably inaccurate at best in a culture whose different components were much less consciously separated than in ours, and the paintings probably took on a value of their own in any case.

There are other aspects of the paintings about which we shall probably never be able to do more than speculate. One of these is the mystery of the so-called tectiforms, abstract or geometric forms that often accompany the animal drawings. These markings—consisting of paired lines, dots, checkers, squares, and even the handprints of the artists—appear repeatedly in deliberate association and definite designs. Moreover, the same sets of markings are found in different caves from different regions. What do they mean? Some archeologists feel they represent some form of primitive written language; others suggest they may be more symbolic in nature, similar to mathematical or musical notation. Whatever their significance, it seems that, like the prehistory of the universe before the Big Bang, we shall likely never know it. No correlative culture survives with which to decipher it. No Rosetta stone will ever be found to explain these strange visual "languages," these extinct modes of expression, forever preserved, forever lost.

But the most compelling thing about the exhibit, aside from the paintings themselves, was the emphasis on the repeated use of these caves. The colored figures which adorn them were not placed in any careful order, but sweep across the walls and ceilings in grand profusion and confusion, crowded together, breaking into one another and overlapping in several layers. It now seems clear that many of these caves were used again and again, not only by several painters in a single tribe, but by several generations of hunter-artists, over a period of hundreds or even thousands of years, exhibiting wide differences in style and perspective. Even when unused sections of the cave were readily available, succeding artists placed their renderings next to or over the previous ones, producing a uniquely cumulative effect and suggesting that the galleries themselves came to have a special meaning for each new group of interpreters. The exhibit commentary, in fact, suggested that, even more than the drawings or the animal spirits they might represent, "these sections of the cave became honored places, as both a source and record of man's perception and his identification with the world."

They were, in other words, places to be visited and
added to, with new visions of new waves of life streaming by over the centuries, places for a laying on of hands
and a rekindling of connections, in imitation and enrich-
ment of nature's own cyclical renewals, places to vouch-
safe and store the fruits of experience, though no eyes
should see them again for millennia to come, and crush-
ing walls of ice, or men themselves, would lay waste to
everything outside during the intervals.

OUTLANDS

has been set in Caledonia, a linotype face designed by American calligrapher and graphic
artist W. A. Dwiggins. This clear and classic
face was inspired by the work of Scotch type-
founders, particularly by the transitional faces
cut by William Martin for Bulmer around 1790.
The display type is Bulmer. The book was set by
Maryland Linotype, Baltimore, Maryland, and
has been printed and bound by Haddon
Craftsmen, Scranton, Pennsylvania.